The Invisible Actor

by the same authors
An Actor Adrift

THE
INVISIBLE
ACTOR

Yoshi Oida and Lorna Marshall

Routledge

Published In the United States of America by Routledge, Inc.

2 4 6 8 10 9 7 5 3 1

Copyright © 1997 Yoshi Oida and Lorna Marshall

Foreword copyright © 1997 Peter Brook

Yoshi Oida and Lorna Marshall have asserted their
rights under the Copyright, Designs and Patents Act, 1988
to be identified as the authors of this work.

First published in the United Kingdom in 1997 by Methuen,
Random House, 20 Vauxhall Bridge Road, London SW1V 2SA

A CIP catalogue record for this book
is available from the Library of Congress

ISBN 0 87830 079 1

Typeset in 10 point Janson Text by
MATS, Southend-on-Sea, Essex
Printed and bound in Great Britain by
Cox & Wyman Ltd, Reading, Berkshire

Contents

Foreword

by Peter Brook

It was during the early days of our work in Paris. The group had
been invited to spend the evening with some musicians in the jazz
club where they worked in Les Halles. Yoshi was beside me as we
struggled to push our way through the only door into the small
room which was crammed to suffocation. We were all squeezed and
hustled on to the stage where the only places that remained were
between the players and the brick wall. The music was not very
interesting, the heat unbearable and yet it was clear that as guests in
full sight of the audience there was no way we could leave before the
end. When, very late indeed, the session finished and we dragged
our hot, sore bodies upright we realised that Yoshi was no longer
with us. How he had escaped unseen remains to this day a mystery
– we knew that he was a flesh and blood creature like us all, so if he
vanished it could not have been by magic, it must have been by art.

My father used to quote to me his old physics professor who
often repeated: 'There are no phenomena that cannot be reduced
to numbers'. In our day, the tragedy of art is that it has no science
and the tragedy of science is that it has no heart. When we read the
title of the great Zen master Zeami's book *Secrets of the Noh* the
Western mind at once thinks of an Orient seen through the murky
smoke of the opium den. In fact, secrets like mysteries are only
vague and romantic when they are unexplored. Yoshi Oida in this
unique book shows how the mysteries and secrets of performance

are inseparable from a very precise, concrete and detailed science learned in the heat of experience.

The vital lessons he passes on to us are told with such lightness and grace that, typically, the difficulties become invisible. Everything seems so simple, but there's a catch: in the East as in the West, nothing is easy.

Paris, 1997

Preface

Yoshi Oida is unique.

His professional career began nearly fifty years ago in Japan. As a child actor, he explored classical Noh theatre, and modern forms of expression, including television. As he grew up, he continued studying and performing various styles of Japanese traditional theatre (Noh, Kabuki, and Gidaiyu storytelling), as well as acting in Western-style plays. He also engaged in experimental work with the playwright Yukio Mishima.

In his late thirties, he left Japan for Europe. He had just met a foreign director called Peter Brook, whose ideas about theatre seemed new and intriguing. Although Yoshi spoke no European language, he packed his bags and got on the plane for Paris. Despite the strangeness of this 'exotic' culture and its unfamiliar approach to creating theatre, Yoshi stayed in France, continuing to explore his craft. Over the years, he became a major force in the work of the Centre International de Création Théâtrale, participating in most of the landmark productions, such as *The Ik*, *The Conference of the Birds*, the *Mahabharata*, *The Man Who*. He has also acted in films, directed plays, and has run workshops for performers throughout the world.

I know of no one else who has this breadth and depth of performing experience. Not just East and West, but also traditional and experimental, text-based and improvised, film and stage, physical and vocal, as actor and teacher and director. It is this extraordinary range of skills and practice that makes him unique; and uniquely qualified to comment on the performer's craft.

Since Yoshi's early training was in the classical theatre traditions of Japan, he often refers to their techniques, approaches, and methods of teaching. A bit of background information may give you a clearer picture of the context for some of Yoshi's comments.

There are two main styles in Japanese theatre: Noh and Kabuki. They came into existence centuries ago, and have maintained their appeal right up until the present day, despite the incursion of Western theatre and television. Although they reflect their historical origins, these styles are not museum pieces, or recreations of a lost tradition. They are living theatre forms with a devoted audience following.

Noh came into existence at the beginning of the fourteenth century, and was codified by its great Master, Zeami. Within the Noh theatre, there are two sub-styles: Noh itself, and Kyogen. Noh is a highly stylised masked theatre, which employs ritualistic dance movements, musical accompaniment, and heightened use of the voice. Its themes tend to be melancholic, concerned with loss, long-ing, and the uncertainty of life and love. Although the costumes are gorgeous, Noh is minimalist in style. It employs an empty stage, formalised gestures, and the use of masks, in order to create a dis-tanced sense of tragic atmosphere (rather than dramatic action). In Noh, there is very little expressed emotion, or direct conflict, and few spectacular effects.

In contrast, Kyogen is very down-to-earth: short farces which explore the trickery of unreliable servants, hypochondriac gods, and general delight in the games of daily life. In a traditional perfor-mance of the Noh theatre, both styles will be used, on the same stage, with Noh and Kyogen plays alternating through the pro-gramme.

In the past, each programme was performed only once in any

given year. No 'season', no repeats. The programme normally consisted of five Noh plays – serious – and four Kyogen plays – comedy – alternating with each other over a single day. While these all-day events are now very rare, their structure still determines the subject matter of the plays. Traditionally, the first Noh play is about gods, the second tells the story of a warrior, and the third has a woman as the main character. The fourth group of plays presents characters (often women) with a greater degree of psychological complexity than in the preceding roles. For this reason, these plays are often described as 'mad woman' pieces, although the actual range of characters included is broader than this title suggests. The fifth and final group tells stories about demons. (In Kyogen, the same categories are used, with the exception of the 'woman' group which does not exist.) The god plays tend to be rather slow and stately, and while the warrior plays may be physically more active, there is little dramatic depth. As you progress into the woman and mad woman categories, there is increasing dramatic complexity and emotional turmoil, and the final demon play is fierce, fast, and relatively spectacular. Nowadays, a Noh programme will include one or two plays from any category.

Kabuki theatre appeared in the seventeenth century, and, like Noh theatre, uses dance, singing, music, and gorgeous costume in its presentation. However, unlike Noh, the objective of Kabuki is to create vivid spectacle which dazzles the audience. The text focuses on dramatic and sentimental events, such as lovers committing suicide, brave (but dispossessed) samurai fighting for their rights, and elegant courtesans at play. Shocking events, erotic beauty, horror, pain, and loss, are all given form through the supreme skill of the actor. And the skill is 'presented' in order to be admired by the audience. In this way its approach is quite different to that of Noh. Rather than the subtlety and indirect suggestion of feeling used in Noh theatre, Kabuki plays are designed to display the actors' physical, vocal, and emotional prowess.

A Kabuki 'season' lasts a month, with a programme that reflects the particular quality of that time of the year – for example, in summer, plays with ghosts ('chilling' stories), or splashing water are often chosen to provide relief from the sweltering heat. Normally, Kabuki performances begin in the morning and continue into the evening, with a number of separate pieces being presented. You can sit there all day, or wander in and out as you wish. You can even bring your lunch into the theatre and munch away during the performance. Within one day's programme, there is no repetition. It isn't a matinee followed by an evening repeat showing, it is a number of separate pieces, one after another. There might be a historical play based on the wars of an earlier epoch, with three distinct acts. Or a comedy, or a more 'psychological' piece, involving conflicts of duty, painful love, and personal self-sacrifice. At the very end is a dance performance which is lighter in mood, although it is often technically dazzling and includes spectacular stage effects.

As well as Noh and Kabuki Theatre, there is also a traditional art of storytelling called Gidaiyu, which was developed in the sixteenth century. It exists as an independent art, but also appears as an accompaniment to Bunraku puppet theatre, and is sometimes (though not always) incorporated into certain plays in the Kabuki theatre. When it is used in Kabuki, it explains and reinforces the dramatic action. In this case, the storyteller sits to one side of the stage, and recounts the events with extraordinary vocal range and emotional passion. A samisen player sits beside him and musically accompanies the storyteller's words in order to heighten the mood even further. The samisen is a long-necked, three-stringed instrument which is plucked to produce sounds that echo the human vocal range.

In these forms of Japanese theatre, 'acting' does not exist as a separate skill; all performance is called either 'dancing' or 'singing' or 'speaking'. The sum of these skills is what Westerners would call 'acting'. This is a reflection of the nature of traditional Japanese theatre, which is a kind of 'total theatre' integrating movement, acting, and heightened vocal production. In the West, theatre has become specialised; actors do the acting, dancers dance, and singers focus on the voice in song. With the exception of musical theatre, very few performers are required to master the skills of other styles of theatre. While there are certain rare individuals who excel equally in singing, dancing, and acting via speech, they are exceptional and are applauded for their versatility. In contrast, a Japanese actor is expected to be proficient in all three areas. This does not mean that a Japanese performer could step into a role at the Royal Opera House in London; Western opera and ballet have developed in their specialised fields over several centuries, and the styles of vocal production and movement are very different in Japan. The important thing to bear in mind is that a traditional performer in Japan is expected to be able to use a wider range of vocal and physical expression than a Western actor, and that the word 'dance' applies to the 'actor'. In Japanese theatre, 'dance' is the visual expression of character, situation, relationship, and emotion, as well as pure movement.

People often ask how I got involved in working with Yoshi. In fact it was somewhat inevitable, since my work in theatre occupied some of the same territory. I had studied with a variety of master teachers in the West and in Japan, and I was asking the same kinds of questions about the nature of performing. Eventually we were introduced to each other, and after many conversations about 'acting' and 'training' (and 'choices' . . . and 'life' . . . etc.), Yoshi asked me to collaborate with him on his autobiography *An Actor Adrift* (Methuen, 1992). And then we decided to write this book.

Over the years of our collaboration, Yoshi and I have spent many hours talking together. On a personal level, these conversations have been incredibly valuable, offering me new ways of viewing myself and my work. However, they are not 'easy' chats. Yoshi very rarely comes out with a direct pronouncement. Instead, he will ask questions, or probe, or tell a seemingly irrelevant story about sword fighting. Nonetheless, even when I disagreed with him, or failed to understand the point of his comments, the questions he raised led me to think more deeply about what I was doing. He made me stop and re-examine my ideas and habitual responses. And eventually I found my own answers to the points he raised. This is how Yoshi works. He will never say, 'If you do A, the outcome will be B.' He will simply ask the question, or suggest the exercise, and leave it to you to discover what can happen.

In working on this book, I have tried to give you a taste of the kind of conversations that I have been privileged to have with Yoshi. There aren't any failsafe recipes for instant success, just questions and suggestions and stories and exercises. Good luck.

Note: The sections in italics are my own comments, usually amplifying or clarifying something Yoshi has said.

Lorna Marshall

Introduction

When I was growing up in Japan, Ninja films were extremely popular, especially with children. Like many of my friends, I loved these films, and went to see them as often as possible.

One of the things that made these films so attractive to children was the 'magical' power of the main character. Ninja warriors could slither up a sheer rockface, or crawl upside-down across a ceiling. They walked on water, and even became 'invisible' at will. Their secret training enabled them to do hundreds of dangerous things, such as sneaking into the enemy camp to spy out the situation, or evading a castle's defences to release their captive friends.

In medieval Japan, Ninja warriors actually existed, although their 'powers' were not magical. They were fighters who specialised in spying, infiltration, and sabotage, using tricks and unusual techniques which enabled them to do things that were seemingly impossible. For example, when they scaled a wall, they had hooks attached to their hands, and they wore small inflatable 'shoes' when walking on water. They wore black clothes as a form of camouflage, and would throw powder into the enemy's eyes when they wanted to make a rapid disappearance. Learning and mastering these techniques took years of training.

Of course, none of these logical explanations for the events ever appeared in the movies. With the help of film technology, the Ninjas were superhuman and magical, imbued with extraordinary powers, able to appear and disappear at will. And they were utterly fascinating to an audience of small children.

Even before I was old enough to go to school, I was enthralled by these films, and told my mother that I wanted to become a Ninja. In particular, I wanted to magically disappear. I kept going on and on about it until, eventually, my mother came up with a solution. She made a sack out of black cloth and gave it to me, saying, 'This is a secret Ninja Magic!'

I immediately pulled the sack over my body, and crouched down on the floor. My mother cried out, 'Where is Yoshi? Where has he disappeared to?'

I was absolutely delighted at my ability to become invisible, and thought, 'At last, I am really a Ninja!'

I then threw off the black fabric and 'suddenly reappeared'. My mother gasped and said, 'Oh, Yoshi! You are here! Why couldn't I see you?'

And we continued this game for some time.

A few weeks later, one of my mother's friends dropped in for a visit. I immediately hid inside the magic Ninja bag, and my mother cried out, as usual, 'Yoshi has disappeared! Where is he?'

Her friend pointed to the bag. 'He's in there!'

At that moment I understood what had been happening, and burst into tears, yelling, 'This magic sack is just a load of rubbish!'

And so I gave up the dream of eventually becoming a Ninja.

The next phase was wigs and makeup.

When there are special celebrations at Shinto shrines, stalls are set up to sell all kinds of goods to the participants, including simple masks and wigs for children. Needless to say, I was fascinated by them, and begged my mother to buy me a samurai wig made of paper, and some black ink which I used to draw fierce, straight eyebrows across my forehead. To increase the impression of heroic courage, I added a beard and moustache. I also experimented with a paper 'geisha' wig and my mother's cosmetics. I slathered my face with masses of white powder until I was completely unrecognisable. A most satisfactory effect.

Next, I pestered my mother to buy me some of the simple plastic or paper masks, which were also on sale at the temples. I raided my parents' wardrobes for clothes. And using my wigs, masks, and costumes, I pretended to be a hundred different people: a lord, a valiant samurai, a beautiful but tragic geisha, and so on. For hours I would parade up and down in front of a mirror, playing at being all these characters.

I can now see that the wigs and makeup that I played with were simply different versions of the original black bag that my mother made for me. A means of vanishing. A way of hiding myself. Disappearing in front of people, rather than performing for them. Of course, I wasn't really 'invisible', but the 'me' they saw was not the 'real me'. Through makeup and masks, I rendered 'myself' invisible.

Given that I preferred to be 'invisible', why on earth did I choose to become an actor, someone who has to reveal himself in public? I have asked myself this question for many years, and now, little by little, I am coming to understand why.

For me, acting is not about showing my presence or displaying my technique. Rather it is about revealing, through acting, 'something else', something that the audience doesn't encounter in daily life. The actor doesn't demonstrate it. It is not physically visible, but, through the engagement of the onlooker's imagination, 'something else' will appear in his or her mind. For this to happen, the audience must not have the slightest awareness of what the actor is doing. They must be able to forget the actor. The actor must disappear.

In the Kabuki theatre, there is a gesture which indicates 'looking at the moon', where the actor points into the sky with his index finger. One actor, who was very talented, performed this gesture with grace and elegance. The audience thought: 'Oh, his movement is so beautiful!' They enjoyed the beauty of his performance, and the technical mastery he displayed.

Another actor made the same gesture, pointing at the moon. The audience didn't notice whether or not he moved elegantly; they simply saw the moon. I prefer this kind of actor: the one who shows the moon to the audience. The actor who can become invisible.

Costumes, wigs, makeup and masks are not enough to achieve this level of 'disappearance'. Ninjas had to spend years training their bodies in order to learn how to become invisible. In the same way, actors must work very hard to develop themselves physically, not simply to acquire skills that can be displayed to the audience, but to be able to disappear.

Master Okura, a famous teacher of Kyogen, once explained the connection between the body and the stage. In Japanese the word for stage is *butai*, the *bu* part meaning 'dance' or 'movement', and *tai* meaning 'stage'. Literally, 'the platform/place of dancing'. However, the word *tai* also means 'body', which suggests an alternative reading: 'the body of dancing'. If we use this meaning of the word *butai*, what is the performer? Okura said that the human body is 'the blood of the dancing body'. Without it the stage is dead. As soon as the performer enters the stage, the space starts to come alive; the 'dancing body' begins 'dancing'. In a sense, it isn't the performer who is 'dancing', but, through his or her movement, the stage 'dances'. Your job as an actor is not to display how well you perform, but rather through your performance to enable the stage to come alive. Once this happens, the audience is carried along and enters the world that the stage creates. They feel that they are in a lonely mountain pass, or in the centre of a battlefield, or anywhere else that exists in the world. The stage contains all these possibilities. It is up to the actor to make them come alive.

Yoshi Oida
Paris, 1997

1 Beginning

CLEANING UP

Before we start doing anything, it is important to clean the working space. Clear it out, get rid of rubbish, and place any essential chairs or props neatly at the sides of the room. Then wash the floor. If actors take the time and trouble to do this at the start of the day's rehearsal, the work tends to go well. In Japan, all the traditions of theatre, religion, and martial arts follow this practice.

But this cleansing is not done in a haphazard way, simply to get rid of dirt, using detergent or even machines. All of the traditional disciplines employ a particular style of floor-washing, using cold water and a cotton cloth, a conscious awareness, and a specific body position. The cloth is rinsed in cold water (no detergent) and then wrung out. This damp cloth is spread on the floor and then the palms of both hands are placed on top. The knees are not on the floor, only the hands and feet, so the body looks like an upside-down 'V'. You then slowly 'walk' forward pushing the cloth across the floor. You normally start at one side of the room, and travel straight across to the other, without stopping. When you arrive at the opposite wall, you stand up, rinse out your cloth, then start again on another 'track'. In this position your hips are strong, and you work the body as well as cleaning the floor. While doing this exercise, you should think only about pushing your cloth, and carefully cleaning. Don't rush, get distracted, or think about other things. Don't chat to other people. All of this is quite difficult, but it is very good training for the concentration an actor needs.

In ancient Indian Buddhist philosophy, there is a concept called 'Samadhi', which refers to a particular level of deep concentration. In a sense, it is quite simple. When you read a book, you just concentrate on reading the book. When you go fishing, you just focus on the movements and quivers of the line itself. When you clean the floor, that's all you do.

In terms of daily life, when you undertake a simple action, try to focus fully on what you are doing. Feel as if you are covered and supported by the whole energy of the universe. Normally our thoughts skitter all over the place: you are washing the floor, but you 'forget' what you are doing, and end up thinking about what happened yesterday, the irritating noise your neighbours make, or worrying about paying the gas bill. In this state it is impossible to be held by the universe's energy. It doesn't really matter what you concentrate on, as long as you concentrate fully. Developing this concentration helps you enter the state of Samadhi. Once in this state, you start to sense the existence of something 'more' than your personal energy. You exist on two levels. For example, you are reading this book now. While you concentrate on 'reading' the words, you are also aware of everything else around you; but the awareness of everything around doesn't disturb you.

I try to extend this exercise into my daily life. When I get up in the morning and clean my teeth, I try to concentrate only on 'cleaning my teeth'. Unfortunately, I always get distracted. I start by carefully focusing on the activity of tooth-brushing, but I usually find myself thinking, 'I mustn't forget to go to the bank . . . And then I must phone so-and-so . . . I wonder if the Metro will be very crowded today . . .' It is extremely difficult to focus only on the act of cleaning; it is easy to be distracted. Nonetheless, actors must be able to go into any activity with one hundred per cent of their being and concentration.

If you view it this way, cleaning up is not simply a 'preparation' for work. The word 'preparation' tends to imply that it is the activity following the 'preparation' that is important. Not in this case. The act of cleaning up itself is useful.

This approach to cleaning is not limited to the place where you will be working. You should also ensure that your body is in the same state of readiness. In Japan, before a major tournament in the martial arts, or prior to a particularly important Noh performance, the fighters/performers will pour cold water over their heads. Not just to get rid of grime, but to purify themselves symbolically. In the same way, it is interesting to note that many of the world's cultures stress the importance of ritual purification. In Islam you wash your feet before entering the mosque, and in Shinto you rinse the mouth and hands before entering the temple; in Christianity, baptism has a symbolic and ceremonial significance. Perhaps these beliefs originated in the need to educate people about hygiene, but they all emphasise the importance of cleaning up as a part of worship.

The value of cleanliness and purity is central to Japanese culture. Of course, the role of washing and cleaning in disease prevention is known across the world, but in Japan there is an additional factor. The act of cleansing oneself and one's surroundings has a spiritual dimension, rooted in the creation story of the Shinto religion. According to this saga, the god Isanagi washed his body to purify himself after a journey to the underworld of the dead. As he cleansed his divine skin, removing the contamination of the underworld, various entities, gods, and land masses were created. In this cosmology, cleansing is linked to creation. It is a positive, powerful act, not simply a means of getting rid of dirt.

In some Shinto sects, the ritual purification of the body takes the form of bathing in the sea, even in the middle of winter. This practice is called misogi. *If it is not done in the sea, it can be undertaken in any body of cold moving water, such as a river, waterfall, or even under the shower. Once immersed, the participant does specific exercises, involving chanting and concentration.*

In terms of daily life, cleansing implies a proper respect for the self, and is an active way of preparing the mind and body for disciplined work. The various martial arts and religious practices all stress the importance of cleaning, not as a preliminary for activity, but as an integral part of the training itself. So they start the day's work with a thorough cleaning of the workrooms, and the body. L.M.

THE NINE HOLES

Preparing the body involves more than getting it clean; you also need to look after it. Especially the 'nine holes'. According to Japanese tradition, the body has nine holes: the two eyes, two nostrils, two ears, one mouth, one hole for passing water, and one hole for defecation. All require attention.

The eye

Since the audience is very aware of the actor's eyes, you should take care of them. For example, it is nice to wash your eyes in tepid water. Place your face in the water, blink your eyes several times, look up, down, right, left, and then move your eyes in a circle. After you have washed the eyes, you can give them a gentle massage. With the eyes closed, place the palms of the hands over the eyes, and push the eyeballs very softly inwards.

In the Kabuki theatre, expressive eyes have always been seen as an essential asset (they are even known as 'million-dollar eyes'). Over the centuries, a number of conventions have been developed where the eyes are used to suggest different emotions; for example, to express sexual charm, you use a sidelong glance, rather than a direct gaze. Because these conventions are an important part of the Kabuki tradition, an actor must be able to fully engage the eyes in performance.

Even outside Kabuki, awareness of the eyes is needed for good acting. For example, you should be able to choose your *me-sen* ('line of eyes'). This includes focus (unfocused, sharply focused, near focus, far focus), as well as direction. There are other traditional tricks, like the convention for 'looking at the moon'. Although, from the audience point of view, it appears that your eyes are focused on the moon, you are actually using your chin to see the moon. It makes the action seem bigger and more true.

Being able to use your eyes well is not confined to the physical world. Remember the phrase, 'The scales fell from my eyes'? The eye can see invisible things as well as concrete objects.

Once upon a time, there was a Master and his student. One day the student approached his teacher and said, 'You have been an excellent teacher, and have taught me many useful things. I would like to show my appreciation for all your help. In my house there is a valuable painting, a treasured heirloom handed down from generation to generation. Personally, I am not much of a connoisseur of paintings, so instead of keeping it for myself, I feel it would be better to give it to you. You could hang it in your house and it might bring you pleasure.'

The Master accepted the painting and hung it on his wall. He sat looking at it, and after a while he turned to the student and said, 'Thank you very much. You have given me fine treasure. In return, I would like to give you a gift of some money.'

The student recoiled, saying, 'No, no! I didn't offer the painting to you in order to get money. I just thought it would be nice for you to have my treasure.'

The Master soothed the student and said, 'Please don't get upset. I also want to say thank you and show my appreciation towards you. I would really like you to take the money.'

The student thought for a moment, and then accepted the money. As he was leaving, he said, 'It makes me very happy to think that my family's great heirloom will be able to stay at your house.'

A few days later, an antique dealer appeared on a visit to the Master. He noticed the painting and exclaimed, 'I am afraid you have been cheated. It is only a copy.'

The Master just smiled, and then replied, 'I already knew that. I haven't hung a painting by a famous artist, I am hanging the good heart of my student. It doesn't matter if the object he gave me is a forgery, it is his heart that is important.'

If you only 'look' at the painting, it is a fake. But if you really 'see' it, it is the generous heart of the student.

There are two sides: visible and invisible. When you deal with the material, you can view it as if it were only 'material'. Alternatively, you can try to work with the material as if it had another meaning or dimension, as if there were something that existed beyond and behind the material form.

The nose

It is very important to get enough air. If your nostrils are blocked, you can manage to breathe in and out using only the mouth, but it is better to take the in-breath through the nose. In addition, there is an old Japanese tradition that connects the nostrils to the 'third eye'. We don't know the exact importance of the 'third eye', but according to traditional belief, having a blocked nose affects the ability to perceive with clarity and to think intelligently. Therefore if you want to ensure that you are fully alert in every sense, keep the nose clear, so that air can freely circulate. (Maybe having a blocked nose is one of the reasons we feel so stupid when we have a cold.)

As well as keeping the nostrils clean (try rinsing them in water), it also helps to massage the sides of the nose. Put your fingers on either side of the nose above the nostrils, and gently move the fingers up towards the bridge of the nose. Continue moving them up and down. It is interesting to note that when we are tired we often instinctively rub our faces, and in doing so, move our hands up and down the side of the nose.

The ears

The next set of orifices are the ears, and they also benefit from the occasional massage. When starting to massage your ears, look for the small bit of cartilage at the front of the ear where it meets the edge of the face. Softly pinch it. Then grasp the earlobe between the thumb and forefinger and move it in a circle. Next, you try to 'expand' the ear by gently pulling it outwards – downwards from the lobe, upwards from the top edge and backwards from the side edge. Then grasp the lobe again and move it freely about. In Japan, it is believed that if you have a big earlobe you will be healthy and rich . . . so keep pulling.

Next, gently press the palm of the hand over the whole of the ear. Keep it there for about three seconds and then sharply release the pressure. Do each ear separately, repeating the process twice. Then, using the palm of the hand, fold the outside edge of the ear inwards. Since it is the palm of the hand that is holding the ear closed, you can use your fingers (which are facing backwards) to gently tap the base of the skull.

The mouth

Next is the mouth. As well as cleaning our teeth, we should pay particular attention to the gums, since healthy gums keep your teeth in place. Here again, massage is a good way to stimulate them. With your mouth closed, place your fingertips on the upper lip just under your nose. Gently tap this area (the base of the gums) with your fingertips, and continue the movement round to the side of the face beneath the cheekbones. Then move your fingers to the chin and continue massaging the gums of the lower jaw in the same way.

Inside the mouth, human beings have three types of teeth: canines, incisors, and molars. Canine teeth are characteristic of animals that eat meat, the incisors belong to eaters of vegetation, while the molars are designed for grinding grain. The percentage of each type of tooth within the mouth gives us an indication of what kind of diet the body is adapted to. One renowned aikido master has noted that out of a total of thirty-two teeth, four are canines, giving a proportion of one in eight. Since only one-eighth of our teeth are designed for meat eating, only one-eighth of our food should be meat.

The anus

In terms of cleanliness, there is nothing particular to say about the two holes for passing water and for defecation. Nonetheless, the region around the anus is important in other ways. In Japan, all the martial arts and theatre traditions place great stress on keeping the anus tight while working. Of course, in daily life you keep it relaxed. Even in performance, it isn't necessarily held clenched all the time. But at the most important moments, when the person needs to strike a powerful blow, or has to use the voice with great power, the anus is held tightly shut. This gives energy to the body and the voice, and provides more strength and focus for your action. On an everyday level, tightening the anus when you attempt to lift or push a heavy object helps protect the body from strain.

When you tighten the anus, you bring your focus to this area of the body. I find that when I do this exercise, I get a kind of 'shock' sensation. Perhaps some kind of 'channel' in my body has been opened, and this permits energy to enter from outside. In a sense, this area is a starting point for energy in the body.

In some sacred Tibetan paintings ('Tantra'), a snake is often shown in the area of the anus. A similar idea appears in an old Chinese Taoist picture of a person sitting down. Beside the base of the spine is a picture of a water-wheel. The wheel resembles a fairground Ferris wheel, with empty buckets going down, dipping into the stream, and then rising upwards filled with water. In this case, the water is a symbol of physical energy, which rises up the spine, promoting inner wellbeing. In the same way, Indian Yoga contains the concept of a 'Serpent of Energy' (called the Kundalini) which is also considered to rise up the spine, in order to enhance spiritual energy.

Similarly, in African dance the area around the anus is very active. Dancers are able to undulate their spine like a snake, and the starting point for this movement is the tip of the tailbone (sacrum) which is located near the anus. The tailbone moves forwards and backwards, and then the rest of the spine follows the impulse upwards. Although this is a purely physical action, I feel that it has another dimension; it can improve the flow of internal energy.

Once we have taken care of our 'nine holes', we can move on to other important parts of the body.

OTHER BODY PARTS

The spine

Any kind of spinal movement (such as the African dance undulations) involves the whole of the body's nervous system. Most of the body's nerves pass from the brain into the limbs via the spine. If the spine is active, and each vertebra can move freely, then the nerves can function better. And so you become more sensitive and aware. In a way, spinal movements act as a kind of massage for the entire nervous system.

For this reason, it is very important to work the spine, so that each vertebra is independently free, and the nerves do not become blocked by muscle. Almost any exercise that involves carefully moving and stretching the spine is good.

Sit comfortably on the ground with your legs loosely spread in front of you, the way a baby sits. Then try to tuck the tip of the tailbone right under your body. Your pelvis will tip backwards. Then take your tailbone the other way, letting it move outwards towards the sky. The pelvis will respond by tilting forwards. Then just keep moving the tailbone in and out for a while. Thinking 'forward . . . back . . . forward . . . back' sometimes helps. Gradually let the movement travel up the spine till the breastbone (sternum) joins in. It will go 'out . . . down . . . out . . . down'. The important thing when doing this exercise is to keep the spine very soft and relaxed. It isn't a big, energetic movement, but you must be precise about beginning the action at the very tip of the tailbone, and then continuing it to the breastbone, so that the entire spine is engaged.

Look at a dog. When it is afraid, its tail tucks in as far as it can. When it is alert, its tail goes straight up. In a sense, a dog shows its emotions through the movements of the tailbone. Tilting the tailbone and then passing that undulation up the spine to the neck and head, somehow makes you feel more 'awake'.

When you work the spine, imagine that you are a huge, sinuous snake. Or imagine that you can feel the energy rising up the spine as you move. When you are simply standing on the spot, imagine that you can sense the earth's energy pouring into the body through the soles of the feet. Whatever you do, don't let it become mechanical. Go with your imagination.

The hara

When Japanese people talk about the 'hara', they are referring to the area of the body that lies a few centimetres below the navel. This is the centre of gravity of the human body, and, in western terms, corresponds to the term 'the belly'. But the Japanese concept of the hara is seen as something more than a physical location; it is the core of the entire self. It is the centre of a person's strength, health, energy, integrity, and sense of connection to the world and the universe. Not only is a strong hara essential for a healthy life, it is impossible to do any kind of physical or spiritual discipline (such as the martial arts, meditation, or theatre) without involving this area. Consequently, training in these fields always incorporates exercises to develop and strengthen the hara. L.M.

One way of preparing and strengthening the hara is to massage it since, paradoxically, a 'strong' hara is soft and malleable. If, when you start to massage it, it feels hard and tense, or there are areas which are tender to the touch, work very gently until it starts to soften. To begin, close your fingers together so that your hand is like a small spade. Using the tips of the four fingers (excluding the thumb) slowly press into the area all around the navel, working in a clockwise direction (i.e. start with your hands to your left, move them down under the navel, then up to your right, and continue the circle until your hands are near your waist). Keep massaging until you have covered the whole of the abdomen area and it feels soft and squidgy like bread dough. If a particular area feels unusually hard, keep gently pressing until it softens.

The hands

Specialists in acupuncture say that there are points located on the sides of the fingers and toes that are directly related to the centre of the body. They are like 'channels' that connect the energy core to the outside world. If you massage these extremities, or give them a 'shock', you are doing the same thing to the inner energy system. In this way, when you stamp your feet or clap your hands for a long period of time, these points on the extremities are stimulated. The 'channels' open, and fresh energy enters from outside.

There is a sect in Japan who clap for half an hour every morning and evening in order to promote their health. The Chinese, too, believe there is a connection between the use of the hands and physical wellbeing. In fact, movements involving contact between the two hands appear in many religious traditions. In Shintoism, you clap the hands together to call the spirits. In Christianity and Buddhism you place the palms together in order to pray.

Place your hands about ten centimetres apart then gently move them a bit closer together (to a distance of five centimetres). Then slowly pull them back to their original position. You might feel a sort of tension between the two palms, rather like elastic, or a kind of magnetic force. Something seems to be there.

You may also have noticed that if you have a stomach-ache, you will subconsciously place your hand on your tummy. Or if you have toothache, you will cradle your jaw in your hands. In fact, any pain causes an almost automatic 'laying-on of hands'. Unconsciously, we know that there is a connection between hand contact and the easing of pain or discomfort. I believe that there is a kind of energy that radiates from the hands that can ease pain or alleviate sickness; and that clapping the hands or placing the palms together serves to stimulate or recharge that energy. Hence the appearance of these practices within religious traditions.

Working with the hands is important in another area. As we all know, old age is often associated with forgetfulness, and even senility. Some Japanese researchers have suggested that part of this problem is lack of 'exercise' for the brain, not just the natural ageing process. To remedy this situation, they have created several undemanding physical exercises. One of them involves making movements with the hand, focusing on the fingers. But just wiggling the fingers about doesn't achieve anything; the imagination must also be involved. So you imagine that you are placing peas in a line, or arranging flowers. It is a simple movement, but because it engages the imagination and connects it to the body, it acts to stimulate the brain. Doing the exercise without imagination is ineffective.

FINAL TOUCHES

In Japanese spiritual training, there are special 'costumes' that you wear when doing exercises. In Shinto, the robes are white, while in Buddhism they are usually red or yellow. In the same way, I think it is nice to put on a special 'costume' when you are working. Your training is not a continuation of ordinary daily life; it is something different. Putting on a 'costume' helps to mark the separation. In the same way, it is a good idea to have a particular space reserved for your personal training.

So when you do your work, you put yourself in a special place which you have cleaned up, you purify your body by immersing it in cold water, you put on a special outfit, and now you are ready to begin work.

2 Moving

The first thing the actor needs to learn is the geography of the body. You start by exploring your spine, then discovering the legs, and finally the arms. In terms of activity, this means that you begin by working in the standing position, and then develop this into descending and rising movements. Next, you explore sitting, followed by walking, which in turn permits you to go anywhere.

Learning the geography of the body is not simply a matter of doing exercises, or acquiring new and interesting movement patterns. It involves active awareness. Look at how you stand normally. Even tiny zones of tension or imbalance affect not only your ease of movement and the way you look from the outside, but also the way you feel emotionally. Every tiny detail of the body corresponds to a different inner reality.

STANDING

In order to sense these subtle shifts, you need to know exactly where your body is at every moment. For example, where are your feet? Of course, they are at the bottom of your legs, but how exactly do they relate to the rest of your anatomy and your inner sensations?

I use four basic positions of the feet as a measure for where the body is. First, stand with your feet touching each other. How does that feel?

Next, place your feet directly below the hip socket. Feel where the thigh bones insert into the hip socket at the top of the legs, and then direct the thigh bones straight down towards the ground. If you do this you will find that your feet are about five to seven centimetres apart if you are a man, and about six to nine centimetres apart if you are a woman. *(People often get this wrong, since they imagine that their hips are much wider than they really are, or they are using the protruding bones at the top of the pelvis as a measure, instead of the place where the leg bone joins the pelvis. L.M.)* Once you find the position, see how it feels.

The next position for the feet is shoulder-width apart. This makes you square in the space.

The final position is larger-than-shoulder width apart. You often find this position in the martial arts, since it is a balanced, active stance.

Once you have discovered these four different positions, decide whether you are placing your feet parallel to each other, or at a forty-five-degree angle. Be exact.

In virtually every theatrical style in the world, emphasis is placed on maintaining a long (but not rigid) spine. There are various ways of achieving this line. One way is by imagining that your sense of self goes down into the earth, while simultaneously feeling that the back of your neck is very long, almost as if your skull is being pulled up into the sky. In addition, the lower end of the sternum is dropped slightly downwards, though not so far as to cause the chest to collapse inwards.

When I was in Africa with Peter Brook, we spent several days travelling across the Sahara desert. In one region, there were no trees, mountains, buildings, telegraph poles or human beings. Just sky, flat earth, and the line of the horizon in every direction. I began to feel lost in the immensity of the world around me.

I started experimenting, trying to find a way of placing my body so that I could exist in this vast emptiness. Standing was no good. It didn't feel right. Then I tried lying down on the surface of the plain, which was covered by tiny pebbles, and looked up at the sky. Lying like this, I felt as if I had become part of the desert soil, absorbed into the earth like a dead man. I had no individual existence. Finally, I tried sitting on the ground with a straight back, and concentrated my energy into my hara. At that moment I suddenly felt as if I had a new kind of existence, suspended between heaven and earth, connecting heaven and earth like a bridge. By trial and error I had found the position that enabled me to exist fully in that particular space.

Stand with your feet apart, the same distance as the width of your shoulders. Then try to imagine that your skin is like a plastic bag. Inside that bag, there is only water. No brain, no heart, no stomach, just water. Clear, crystal-clean water. Without closing your eyes, you watch the water. Eventually, it starts to move. To the front, to the right, to the left, to the back. It is a beautiful soft movement, just like the water. At a certain moment, when you have established a clear sense of your body as water, you try to feel the earth's gravity. Some force comes from the centre of the earth and it invites you to descend; down, down, but your flesh remains water. Your head becomes heavy, your shoulders become heavy, and your arms become heavy because of the force of gravity. Gradually you sink towards the floor until you find yourself in the squatting position, with head and arms relaxed.

Then imagine that there are three threads that link your body to the sky. One of these threads connects to the top of your skull, and the other two are connected to your wrists. The three threads start to pull you upwards into the sky, until you find yourself standing upright again, with the arms suspended in the air. As if this bag of water were hanging in the air. Then once again you feel the pull of the earth's gravity, the threads disappear, and your arms and head sink downwards, to be followed by the rest of the body. You continue this exercise, constantly moving between the sky and the earth, while the body remains water. As you repeat the movement it gradually speeds up. Towards the end, you forget about the threads to the wrists; there is only one thread, which connects to the top of the skull. You keep going up and down for a while, without any effort, and then eventually you slow down and come to a stop in the standing position. You feel as if you are suspended and balanced between the two forces of the sky and the earth.

PRACTISING

A Zen master once likened humans to puppets held up by strings. At the moments of birth and death these strings are drawn tight or suddenly severed. When people die, he said, the string is cut and, with a sound, the puppet collapses.

It is the same for actors when performing on the stage. You are a puppet held up and manipulated by the 'strings' of your mind. If the audience sees the 'strings', the performance isn't interesting. Although you need to maintain a powerful concentration at all times, during action and during stillness, this must never be visible. The audience should never see you concentrating.

On the other hand, if your concentration wavers, it is as if the strings of the puppet have become slack. The actions are jerky, and the audience becomes aware that they are watching a puppet, rather than being convinced that they are seeing a real living being. In the same way, if the 'thread' of the actor's concentration becomes slack, the performance doesn't work. When the 'thread' remains taut yet invisible, the performance will look truthful and unmechanical: completely alive.

This kind of 'tension of the thread' is not only used on the stage; it also exists as we 'act' in daily life. As you go about your ordinary activities, you should try to maintain a deep awareness in your mind, a kind of 'tension of the soul'. Each act in daily life must be undertaken with a 'tight thread', bringing a full consciousness of your whole self to every moment of every hour.

As an actor, it is essential that you engage and exercise your imagination wherever possible. Ideally, any physical exercise that you do should also become an exercise of the imagination, not just working your body. There is another benefit as well. If you do a simple exercise such as knee bends and think only about the muscles involved, your legs will quickly become heavy and painful, and the movement becomes hard labour. But if you use the image of strings and moving between sky and earth, the action becomes easier, and you have a focus for your inner concentration.

When you are doing an exercise, you tend to think, 'Oh, this is just an exercise. If I make a mistake, it doesn't really matter.'

However, if you make a mistake on the stage, you have to keep going and attempt to cover up the error. You can't stop and try again. In fact, you really can't afford to make mistakes at all. Traditional actors who constantly 'test' their work in front of a real audience are used to this problem, and their work has a definite focus and immediacy, even when they are practising. All actors should think this way when they train.

Whenever you practise, imagine that you are doing your exercises in front of an audience. It suddenly becomes important that you engage fully, and avoid sloppiness. In this way, the quality of your work will improve, and the training will be genuinely useful. If you think that you are 'only doing an exercise', the work will be of little value, irrespective of how well you perform it.

You can even practise this technique in daily life. Imagine that you are on the stage and that people are watching. Of course, you don't need to portray a character, or do anything fancy. Just be yourself. Be natural. As you get used to it, you will probably find that your consciousness begins to change. You remain aware of the outside world, and don't become totally lost in your activities. When you 'perform' in this way, you are completely yourself, and at the same time you are aware of watching yourself. You maintain two states: self-subjective and self-objective. Imagining you are being watched by an audience produces this kind of split awareness, but in addition the body learns something when it thinks it is being 'observed'. This isn't the same as narcissism or exhibitionism, but your body simply learns to become accustomed to being watched. In this way, when you actually go in front of a real audience, your body is used to it, and you aren't suddenly faced with a new and terrifying experience. If you are not accustomed to being observed, suddenly stepping on stage and feeling the eyes of the audience will affect you. Your body will react differently, and your feelings will probably not be very free. But if you imagine the presence of an audience either in daily life, or when you are doing exercises, you will become used to this scrutiny and it will be familiar and therefore less threatening when you encounter it for real. Your imagination helps you here.

DIRECTIONS OF MOVEMENT

In everyday life, we tend to keep our attention focused inside our skin. We move the body around, pick up objects, avoid bumping into chairs, and negotiate our way along crowded streets. And during all this activity, we rarely think about where our body is actually situated in the space around us.

However, the actor's body exists within the unique space of the theatre, and it needs to 'expand' in order to fill it. As well as being aware of your skin and bones, you must be able to sense all of the directions that surround your body. Just stand somewhere in the performing space and ask yourself the following questions. Where is the front, the back, the side, up, and down? And in relation to the audience, are you facing directly towards them, or are you standing on a slight diagonal?

This sense of space can be codified into eight directions. In relation to the audience these are: directly front, directly back, to the sides on the right and left, and the four diagonals in between. This creates a kind of eight-pointed star, which forms a clear pattern in space: a basic template for action, although other geometric patterns, such as the circle, can be used. As well as helping the actor gain a sense of the body in space, it also creates a very clean stage picture from the audience point of view.

There is an exercise that helps you experience the eight-direction 'star'. Stand facing the front (the audience), with the feet placed in parallel position, about hip width apart. The right foot steps directly forwards into a lunge, and the whole body goes with it. As you step, the arms also swing forward till they reach shoulder height. When you arrive, your right leg will be bent, while the left will be nearly straight. The weight will be mainly on the front leg, while the spine remains straight and upright.

Then the whole body swivels 180 degrees to face the back, without changing the position of the feet. You just pivot on the spot turning your whole body, without lifting either foot. You end up facing the back wall, away from the audience with the left foot in 'front'. As you pivot, you let the weight swing forward on to the left leg, ending in a lunge position with the left knee bent. During the turn the arms swing back and then forward again to this new 'front'.

Then the whole process starts again from this position: the right foot steps out again, this time directly to the side on your right. It moves from 'behind' the left leg, directly to the new position, becoming the new 'front' leg, facing stage right. Then you follow with another 180-degree swivel to the opposite side ending up facing stage left. You have now traced the front, back, right side, and left side arms of the star.

The pattern then continues to the four diagonals. Step the right foot 'forward' to the right-hand diagonal facing away from the audience (in theatre parlance: upstage right). Pivot 180 degrees, so that you are facing the audience, on the downstage left diagonal. Now, step the right foot forward to the downstage right diagonal, facing the audience and then pivot so that you are facing away from the audience, on the upstage left diagonal. You are now ready to start the whole 'star' again, by stepping directly towards the audience with your right foot. The sequence is always 'step right foot forward, pivot, step right foot forward, pivot'.

Each time you change direction, the whole body turns to the new 'front', not just the feet. This helps you gain a real sense of the stage space in relation to the audience.

In a stylised performance, this star-shaped floor pattern is very clearly indicated, but it isn't necessary to be quite so obvious when you are working realistically. You can stay aware of the eight directions, and base your performance on them, without becoming mechanical. Your actions will still look very natural, while at the same time retaining a quality of clarity and spaciousness. In addition, movements involving the spatial planes work the body on a more fundamental level. They help you to sense your basic human connection to the world around you.

In terms of our relation to the earth, we know that prostrating the body on the ground has a profound effect. It can bring you into a state of deep calm and inner balance. I don't know how it happens, but it is very powerful. Which is probably why so many religions use it.

Even in daily life, it is useful to think about how and where you place your body. According to Japanese tradition, when people's bodies are being prepared for burial, they are always placed with their heads to the north. Statues of the reclining Buddha always have the body lying on the right side while the head points to the north. There is also a belief in Japan that you cannot sleep well if your head points to the west. The logic of this is based on the direction of the earth's spin. If you sleep with your head travelling in the same direction as the spin (i.e., to the east), the sensation is different from that where your head is oriented to the west, in which case you are travelling feet first. So if you have to sleep with your bed parallel to the equator, place your head to the east. However, the most recommended position for sleeping is with your head facing towards the nearer pole, in other words to the north, if you live in the northern hemisphere. I suppose if you are living in the southern hemisphere, you should sleep with your head to the south.

I don't really know if all these traditional beliefs are true or useful, but it is clear that lying in different positions produces different inner sensations. We all know that lying on our right side feels quite different from lying on our left, and we each have definite preferences about our sleeping positions.

In a sense, we exist in a web of time and space. Our bodies are situated at the centre of north, south, east, west, up, down, right, left, past, future, birth, and death.

SITTING

The next position to consider is sitting. In the West, actors usually base their movements on the standing position, or sit in chairs, rarely descending to the floor. But in Japanese theatre, the floor sitting position is frequently used in performance. Using the floor opens up a greater visual field for the audience, although how you move between the sitting and standing positions is important. One simple thing to consider, if you sit on the floor, is to choose a position that offers the greatest potential range of easy movement, especially the ability to rise to standing.

A common position is sitting with your legs crossed 'tailor fashion', but this is quite limited. It is difficult to take the next step of standing up or moving forward with any degree of smoothness. The position is very 'established'; you can sit in it for a long time, but it is not related to activity. Other positions, such as sitting on your heels with either your toes extended (Japanese style) or curled under (as frequently seen on ancient Greek pottery) offer more freedom. In these positions, your body is in a greater state of readiness for action, and can move quickly upwards. If you want to retain the freedom to initiate activity from the floor, it is easier if you start from one of these positions.

A useful exercise is to spend some time just simply exploring how your body functions in the act of moving between sitting and standing. In particular, try doing these actions in extreme slow motion, for example taking five minutes to sit down. In this way, you will discover the most practical way of proceeding; how you hold the head, the balance of the body, where you shift your weight, which leg does most of the work, and so on. You should also engage your imagination as a part of the exercise. When you descend you could use the earlier image of the earth's gravity pulling your body towards the floor; and for standing up, that you are a puppet suspended from the sky by a thread. Or create some other image.

RELAXING

As part of understanding your body, you need to know the difference between being relaxed and being tense, and how to control each state. In practice, this is quite hard to achieve, especially if someone says to you, 'Just relax! Come on, relax!' You just don't know where to begin.

One way is to fully clench the muscles of the body. Become as tense as possible, so you know what 'tense' really feels like, and then suddenly release the muscles. At that moment you will get a sense of what the opposite of 'tense' feels like.

This idea of opposites can be valuable in other areas. For example, in order to jump high, you must bend the knees deeply. In order to strike a drum with your hand you must first move the arm away from the instrument. And the further away you move your arm, the stronger the blow on the drumskin, and the louder the noise.

There was once a man who had been studying Noh theatre for many years. Eventually his teacher said to him, 'You have been working hard for a very long time. I think you have learned enough to be worthy of receiving the hidden traditions of acting in the Noh theatre. So here is a copy of our secret book.'

The student was overjoyed to be given this privilege, humbly thanked his teacher, and immediately ran to find a quiet place where he could read this precious book. He opened the cover. The first page was blank. The next page was also blank, and the next, and so on until the very final page. On this page was written, *Place your strength in your little finger.*

The student was completely bemused. He couldn't understand what this meant.

But the same advice is given in the martial arts. When a samurai holds a sword, he does not grip it with his hand, or arm, or even his thumb. He concentrates on his little finger. In this way, his movements are both strong and free.

If you try this yourself with any kind of activity, you will find that it is effective. Pick up a cup as you would normally, using your hand and fingers, but concentrating on placing the strength in the little finger. In fact, it is your little finger that holds the cup; the other digits are simply there for balance and guidance. It feels very different. For some reason, engaging this finger enables the energy to circulate more effectively. In addition, if, when picking up the cup, you focus your strength in your arm the shoulder will tend to tighten, and this looks very tense on stage. If you focus your strength elsewhere, nobody can see it in operation, and your movements will seem more effortless.

Another Noh master phrased it slightly differently. He said, 'The secret is in the little finger and the arch of the foot. You place your force there. I cannot tell you the reason, but this is the secret.'

In fact, it is impossible to tense the muscles strongly in those areas, but, by thinking about these regions, you have directed your attention away from your head, or neck, or legs (where muscular tension creates visible problems for the actor).

WALKING

When you observe someone who naturally walks well, they don't seem to move from their hips to the head. You have a sense that the legs are the only things in action, while the upper body is 'quiet'. This is not the 'quiet' of rigidity or muscular effort; it is the 'quiet' of relaxed freedom. The body is tranquil; even the internal organs are quiet. In this way, you can easily walk a long distance without becoming tired.

You can see this in action in the Noh theatre. The actor's body itself doesn't move, instead it seems to be effortlessly transported about the stage by the feet. The performers look as if they are 'sitting' very comfortably in their body, and as a result their movements are well balanced. The muscles work in a relaxed but powerful way; but part of the ease of action is a consequence of what is happening inside.

When you study Noh, you are constantly reminded about the importance of the hara, and this area is held open. As a result, internal energy can accumulate, which in turn keeps you physically centred and well balanced. A good actor is comfortably stable; not rigid like a tree, but soft like water.

Try the following exercise. Stand calmly, facing a partner. You are relaxed and receptive. Your partner tries to knock you off-balance by quickly pushing either the right or left shoulder, or the right or left hip (first one part, and then another; not all at the same time). Your partner attempts to catch you off-guard, so that you can't anticipate which part will be hit. If you are well centred, there is nothing your partner can do to knock you over. No matter how hard he or she pushes, you simply absorb the impact and then tranquilly return to the upright position. You do not resist the push with muscular tension. Instead you are poised and receptive, and therefore able to simply absorb whatever happens.

When the hara is open, your internal energy increases, making you more balanced. Moreover, since the focus for the voice is under the navel, the open hara is important here. Conversely, if you 'open' your chest, you become unbalanced.

Even in everyday life, if you walk around with your energy focused in the top half of the body, you will get tired very quickly.

If you drop your energy down into the hara, you will be able to continue for much longer, and feel less fatigue.

Try to 'walk naturally'. Just walk without adding anything extra. You will notice that your walk is unique; absolutely individual. Each person tries to be 'natural', but their 'natural' walk is very complex and reflects their character. One person might swing the right arm more than the left one. Someone else carries their left shoulder higher than the right, or tilts the head slightly to one side. These small differences are what makes each person unique. Sometimes these idiosyncrasies are charming, sometimes they can appear rather unattractive. But if you look at animals, these personal differences don't occur. A Japanese cat moves in much the same way as a European or an African cat.

Any human body is heavily influenced by its culture (country, class, social group, etc.). The personal history of the individual also shapes the physicality. And while it is nice to have a body that is absolutely unique, actors have to be able to play a wide range of different characters. They need to be able to 'drop' their personal body in order to discover and incarnate the character's body. Each character that you play is a unique individual, and you have to search for his or her particular body.

In order to make this process easier, it is helpful to start from a 'neutral' body: one which is simply 'human' and does not reflect your individual history. This is the body you were born into, with nothing extra added. It isn't easy to reclaim, but once you have a sense of this body, you can start to move and discover how to 'walk naturally'.

On the simplest level, when you walk, try to keep the two feet even. Step right, then left, giving each foot an equal weight and rhythm, and ensuring that the body is straight and evenly balanced. Try to find just the essence of 'walking'.

One Japanese tradition recommends that parents should inspect the shoes of their prospective son-in-law, before giving permission for their daughter to marry. If the back of the heel is worn down, it is a very bad sign, indicating that he is lazy. In this event the young man should be shown the door. If the would-be bridegroom has shoes that are worn down at the front, it is seen as a good sign. He may be hasty, but the body is healthy and energetic, and so there are strong hopes for future prosperity. In this case, permission to wed would be forthcoming.

This philosophy also appears in the martial arts, where the weight is carried by the front of the foot. It is also the same in Noh theatre. This doesn't mean that you dance about on your toes all the time, nor is it the ballet style of walking (toe to the floor followed by the heel). Rather, as with normal walking, the heel makes initial contact with the floor, but the weight is rapidly transferred to the ball of the foot. It is important to keep the weight of the body forward, instead of letting it sit back on the heels. Although the weight is carried on the front of the foot, the action of walking is initiated in the hara. You walk from your 'centre', and your toes 'grab the earth' to propel you strongly onwards. If you use this slightly forward position when standing, you will be able to react more quickly and to move more freely.

One day a great samurai went to watch a Noh performance given by an actor of high reputation. He returned from the theatre and a friend asked him what he thought of the actor. The samurai replied, 'He's really very good. His performance was perfect: he didn't leave a single opening for attack.'

Once you get the sense of simply walking, you can start to think about turning corners. Oddly enough, turning right and turning left do not feel the same. Theoretically, they should be identical since the action is identical, but somehow the inner sensation is different. (It is also interesting to note that most people veer slightly to the left when they walk with their eyes closed.) I don't know why each direction produces a different inner sensation, but this phenomenon definitely exists. In the Noh theatre, it is recognised, and has led to the creation of a particular convention. When the actor has to start some activity, such as going off to fight, he turns to the right. If he is returning home, or feeling sad, he turns to the left. For you the inner feeling might be quite different. Experiment and see.

TASTING

When doing all these exercises, it is important to remind yourself to 'taste' the movements. Doing them mechanically doesn't mean very much. You must try to notice the different sensations within the body. What is the exact difference between the arms being vertical and their being horizontal? And it isn't only the larger movements that you investigate in this way. Just use one hand. Hold it open, and then close it: the sensation is not the same. Then move the hand about, turning the palm towards you, then away from your body. Make a fist, then open the hand, starting from the little finger. This feels different from opening the fist by first releasing the thumb. These are tiny movements, but they all affect your interior in different ways. As you work, you must remember that you are not a machine, and that you need to find out exactly how each shift in your body affects your inner being.

But when I talk about these changes in 'sensation', I am not referring to either emotion or psychology; it is something more fundamental: the body's own direct response. It is important to understand that acting isn't only emotion, or movement, or the actions that we commonly recognise as being 'acting'. It also involves this fundamental level: the basic sensations of the body.

One of my masters said, 'As an actor, you shouldn't be a theorist. Don't be too logical or rely on intellectual understanding. Learn through the body.'

Maybe even writing this book is a bad idea, since it is an intellectual exercise. The main thing to remember is that you need to understand acting with your body, not your brain. The act of performing is not the same as intellectual understanding or theory.

All of Yoshi's work places great emphasis on the body. When he teaches, he starts the day with strong physical exercises which last for a long time, often up to two or three hours. While many other practitioners appear to do the same thing, Yoshi's approach is different. For Yoshi, the purpose of physical work is not to warm up, or to become strong and flexible, or to learn how to move 'well' (these are side benefits). It is not a preparation for acting. For him, working physically enables the performer to gain a deeper understanding of fundamental processes: through the body to learn something beyond the body.

To achieve this, you need to be fully 'present' inside your flesh, at all times, even when you are doing exercises that aren't related to Yoshi's work. L.M.

3 Performing

JO, HA, KYU

I often ask a group of actors to sit in a circle, close their eyes, and clap their hands together, while trying to keep the sound in unison. No leader, no pre-fixed rhythm. Every time, once the group has come together, the clapping will start to imperceptibly speed up until a climax is reached. Then it will slow down again (though not as slow as the original starting point), and once more start to speed up until it reaches a second climax. And so on.

Six hundred years ago, the Japanese Noh master, Zeami, said, 'Every phenomenon in the universe develops itself through a certain progression. Even the cry of a bird and the noise of an insect follow this progression. It is called Jo, Ha, Kyu.'

Motokiyo Zeami (AD 1363–1443) was responsible for the creation of the Noh theatre. He welded together two earlier styles of performance, Sarugaku and Dengaku. Sarugaku (literally 'monkey music') was a form of popular entertainment, using tricks, comedy and acrobatics. Dengaku ('field music') had its origin in the songs and dances that were performed as part of agricultural ritual.

As this new art emerged, Zeami refined its subject matter, style of presentation, and acting techniques. In order to pass on his insights to following generations of actors, he wrote several treatises. These were

handed down in secret, within the families of the Noh theatre. Only in
1908, when a collection of these writings accidentally appeared in a second-
hand bookshop, did the information become available to the general public.
Although Zeami's books were written hundreds of years ago, his ideas are
fascinating, and completely relevant to modern (and Western) actors.

Although Japanese theatre is heavily stylised in terms of performance,
many of the conventions are actually based on an accurate observation of
natural patterns. Zeami noticed one of these patterns, a rhythmic
structure called Jo, Ha, Kyu. (The word jo literally means 'beginning' or
'opening', ha means 'break' or 'development', and kyu has the sense of
'fast' or 'climax'.) In this structure, you start slowly, then gradually and
smoothly accelerate towards a very fast peak. After the peak, there is
usually a pause and then a recommencement of the acceleration cycle. A
new Jo Ha Kyu. This is an organic rhythm which can easily be observed
in the body's build-up to sexual orgasm. Almost any rhythmic physical
activity will tend to follow this pattern if left to itself.

This rhythm of Jo, Ha, Kyu is quite different from the Western idea of
'beginning, middle, end', since the latter tends to produce a series of 'steps'
rather than a smooth acceleration. In addition, the concept of 'beginning,
middle, end' usually only refers to the overall dramatic structure of the play,
while Jo, Ha, Kyu is used to support every moment of a performance as well
as its structure. In Japanese theatre, each play has Jo, Ha, Kyu, each act and
scene has Jo, Ha, Kyu, and each individual speech will have its own internal
Jo, Ha, Kyu. Even a single gesture such as the raising of an arm will com-
mence at a certain speed and end at a slightly faster rhythm. The degree of
acceleration will vary; sometimes it is quite clear to the onlooker, sometimes the
shift in tempo is so slight as to be invisible, but it is always there. The sense of
onward progression is never absent. Sometime the surface of the action slows
down, or stops completely, and there is no visible Jo, Ha, Kyu; nonetheless, the
development of Jo, Ha, Kyu is still happening, this time on an internal level.

From the audience's point of view, there is a real sense of being
constantly carried forwards. There may be a huge variety of surface
rhythms within any given performance, but the audience will never sense
that the action has 'slackened off'.

There is another factor. Since the Jo, Ha, Kyu pattern also exists within the body of the onlooker, the audience experiences a sense of organic 'rightness' when actors use this rhythm. The bodies of the actors and the bodies of the watchers become connected, and it feels as if they are sharing the same journey.

Many Western performers use the Jo, Ha, Kyu rhythm subconsciously. They can sense when a performance is getting 'bogged down', when you need to 'pick it up' and 'keep it moving'. They know that 'keeping it going' feels right. What Japanese classical theatre has done is to recognise and codify this pattern, and to consciously apply it to all aspects of performance. It isn't anything 'exotic' or applicable only to Japanese theatre; it's a useful tool for any performer. L.M.

Jo, Ha, Kyu isn't just an esoteric theatrical concept, but a rhythm that the audience senses in their flesh and bones. If the actor or director is not aware of this fact, you could end up with a production where there is a contradiction between the inner rhythms of the audience and the production. In this case the audience cannot relax and allow themselves to be carried into the performance. Of course, it is possible to deliberately aim at working against the audience's organic rhythm. You could make the whole production very slow, or very fast all the time. It will certainly shake the audience out of their natural rhythm, and they may perceive the production as being very 'artistic'. In this case, their enjoyment is intellectual rather than instinctive. For myself, I prefer theatre that involves me in a physical and organic way, rather than appealing to my intellect alone.

It is virtually impossible to 'be' natural on stage all the time. Nonetheless, it is essential to 'seem' natural (from the audience's point of view) at every moment of the performance. Since Jo, Ha, Kyu is a fundamental pattern that the audience unconsciously recognises as 'truthful', using it helps your acting appear more organic and 'natural'. In addition, working in a 'real' rhythm that fits what you are doing, somehow makes it easier for genuine feelings to emerge spontaneously. In this way the action becomes more truthful for both the audience and the actors.

Time

The first moment of the play is very important. For directors, the problem is how to start the performance. For an actor, the difficulty is arriving in front of the audience for the first time. This is a really hard moment. While it is true that leaving the stage is also a bit tricky, the initial appearance is more important. When you drive a car, you put it into first gear, and you have to pump the accelerator. In the same way, you need a lot of energy for the start of your performance. Finding a strong beginning enables the Jo, Ha, Kyu of the whole play to get off to a strong start. (Curiously enough, I discovered that finding a good ending helps you to find a good beginning.)

The arts of painting and sculpture are expressed in space while theatre employs time and space. A performance (as opposed to a script) exists only in the moment you actually see it. And the nature of that exact moment is constantly changing, as the play unfolds, new moment by new moment. Even if you go back to see the play again, no two performances are exactly identical. The precise moment you are seeing will never be repeated again.

Because the dimension of time is central to theatre work, it is important to become aware of its 'movement'. For example, you do an action, such as wiggling your little finger. That is the action, but how do you develop it in time? One way of 'developing' this action is to repeat it. But is this repetition a 'development' or simply a continuation? One way forward is to ask your body how it wants to develop the action. Maybe the movement gradually gets bigger, or moves into another part of the body. The important thing here is to ask the body where it wants to go next. It is not an intellectual decision in which the brain tells the body what to do. It is a matter of listening to the body's own sense of time.

When you try this exercise, you can use any part of the body (finger, hip, head, knee, or whatever) but start very small, with just a tiny movement in one isolated spot. Start by repeating the action several times. Keep repeating and then ask the body how it wants to develop this pattern. Maybe all the fingers will join in the rhythm, and then the arm. Or perhaps the other hand will get involved, and then the leg. You are keeping the original dynamic quality of the movement, but it is developing by becoming bigger and spreading further through the body. In this case, the development is through enlargement.

Or you can begin with a large movement, and 'develop' it by letting it become smaller and more focused. This is development through reduction.

Another way of developing the work in time is through transformation. The physical action suddenly shifts into a completely new pattern. Again this is not an intellectual decision, where the mind initiates a change by saying something like 'I am waving my hand up and down, now I think I will flick my leg.' Rather, you find yourself in a particular body position or doing an action, and then you ask the body, 'Do you want to move to another position or action? Where do you feel would be nice?' It is a body decision. You must find the body's response. If it isn't done this way, it can look very artificial and contrived.

In all aspects of performance you need this process of development in time. You start with something specific and then you need to find ways of letting it grow from moment to moment. The process of development might take the form of enlargement, reduction, or transformation, but it is always development. Not just 'change'. When you impose a 'change' on a scene, this is acting from the head, it doesn't come from your organic sense of time and space. And the audience can sense the difference.

As we noticed with Jo, Ha, Kyu, the body wants to develop the action (clapping the hands, for example) through gradually speeding up. Then, once the sound reaches a certain point (where the hands are clapping very fast), the body wants to slow down for a bit, and then it starts to gather speed again. And so on. Jo, Ha, Kyu is a rhythm the body knows and likes. It isn't an imposed pattern. Every time you find yourself in a certain position or movement pattern, the body will want to do something in response. You must learn to listen to what the body wants to do.

'Listening to the body' requires training, since it isn't the same as doing 'whatever you want'. It is specific and very subtle. The body that you listen to must be alive. A body that isn't alive can't tell you what it wants. You ask a question, but there is no response. It doesn't know what it wants; it is a 'dead' body.

As actors, our whole life follows Jo, Ha, Kyu. We sleep at night, start to wake up in the morning, get energetic through the afternoon and evening, and then return to sleep. We pass through the cycle of spring, summer, autumn, and winter. We start our career as slow beginners, develop increasing mastery of our craft, and then become 'old pro's'. We are born, we live, we die.

Space

As you work, you gain a greater awareness of your body, its preferences, and begin noticing how even tiny physical changes can affect your inner states. You start to really inhabit your body, and see how the subtlest shift in your body affects your inner landscape. Sensing this mysterious connection, moment by moment, as we perform, is quite wonderful.

This moment-by-moment discovery is fascinating, but as actors we want to go further. We want to create for the audience a sense that there is something 'more' behind each of these moments; that what we are doing and saying is somehow the distillation of a longer period of time, or a deeper level of human experience.

In ancient times, the shogun Hideyoshi was the patron of a famous tea-ceremony master called Rikyu. One day Hideyoshi said to Rikyu, 'I have heard that you have some beautiful flowers in your garden this spring. I would like to see them.'

Rikyu agreed, and invited the shogun to visit the following day. Full of anticipation, Hideyoshi arrived at the garden gate. But as he entered, he was shocked to see that that there wasn't a single blossom in sight. Rikyu had cut all the flowers. Hideyoshi asked, 'Why have you done this? I came especially to see the flowers!'

Rikyu replied, 'Don't worry, come into the inner garden.'

The two men entered the inner garden, where once again every single flower had been removed. The shogun was becoming more and more angry at what seemed to be the deliberate refusal of his request. He turned to Rikyu and demanded, 'Why have you done this?'

And Rikyu calmly responded, 'Please don't worry. Just come into my Tea Ceremony House.'

The shogun and the tea-ceremony master entered the tiny hut in the centre of the garden. In the corner of the small room was one lone flower. It was an extremely beautiful flower, and as he admired it, Hideyoshi understood Rikyu's actions. In a way, this single perfect flower was more beautiful than the thousands of blooms that had existed in the garden. It was only a single blossom but it suggested more than that. It represented the totality of 'Flower'. It became the essence of all flowers, not only those in Rikyu's garden that spring, but all flowers, everywhere.

When I was in a Zen monastery, the priest suggested that when I picked up a plate, or held a cup of tea, I should try to imagine that it weighed four or five kilograms. I don't know why, but if you imagine that the object is very heavy, the relationship between you and it becomes very important from the audience's point of view. In daily life you don't worry very much about the things around you; you worry only about yourself. Your relationship to your cup and plate is very ordinary. But if you hold the object as if it is extremely heavy, you are forced to become aware of your particular relationship to it. And the relationship is no longer 'everyday', it starts to suggest 'something more'.

There are some techniques that help you manifest this quality, without slipping into crass over-acting. For example, the scene requires you to walk for two metres: fine, that's what you do; but as an actor, your inner intention is to move towards the horizon. If you sit, you feel that you are lowering your body into the centre of the earth. When you stand up, you imagine that you are rising towards the centre of the universe. In daily life, you work with real distances. The chair is two metres away, so your intention is simply to walk those two metres. When you sit, you take the easiest way down. But on stage, you are playing with the full breadth of life, and so your actions have to be something more than just 'walking two metres' or 'sitting down'. You don't 'demonstrate', or try to make the audience see that these actions are somehow 'Deeply Significant'. You simply imagine that the space you are working with is bigger. When you walk across the stage, in your imagination, you go to the horizon.

Also, if you think about the object in this way, you tend to automatically engage the entire body in the act of lifting. On stage, it is very important that the whole body be involved in whatever you are doing, even if the visible movement is quite tiny. You don't need to demonstrate that the object is heavy (as in mime), but in your imagination it weighs a lot.

In the same way, an actor's body is an 'object' that can be made more resonant and significant. You have a daily body that goes to the shops in the morning and does the washing up after a meal. You also have a performing 'object' that can speak of other levels of human experience. As you train your body, it is important to remember that you are training the 'actor's body', which is 'bigger' and more resonant than the 'daily body'.

A great tea-ceremony master was sent to Tokyo by his lord, to visit the shogun. In order to help him travel more safely, the lord instructed the tea-ceremony master to wear a sword. Normally, only samurai warriors were permitted to wear a sword, but since the costume of a samurai and a tea-ceremony master were the same, the lord hoped to protect his servant by passing him off as a dangerous warrior who nobody in their right mind would choose to annoy. Naturally he didn't have a clue how to fight, but the lord hoped his martial appearance would be enough to deter any attackers.

So the master strapped on the sword and started walking towards Tokyo. On the way, he accidentally jostled another (real) samurai. Enraged by the insult, the real samurai immediately challenged the other to a duel. The tea master apologised profusely, and explained that he wasn't really a samurai, merely posing as one on his lord's instructions. The samurai refused to believe his story and declared, 'It makes no difference. You are carrying a sword and so you have an obligation to accept the challenge.'

The tea-ceremony master realised that he was facing his death, and replied, 'I don't know how to fight, so if you want to kill me just go ahead.'

The samurai refused to do this since it would have been dishonourable to kill a man who had never drawn a sword. They discussed the problem and agreed to postpone the duel for an hour. This would give the tea-ceremony master the time to prepare himself. He wanted to die with a little style and dignity, holding the sword properly. He wanted to learn at least that little bit of technique.

So the master went to a martial arts school nearby and told the head teacher the whole story. But instead of giving him a lesson in sword-holding, this teacher asked the master to perform a tea ceremony. He agreed, thinking, 'This will be the last ceremony I ever do in my life.'

When the ceremony was finished, the martial arts master said, 'Very good. You are perfect. You don't need to learn the techniques of fighting, since you are already fully prepared for battle. Your comportment as a samurai is perfect, so all you will need to do is to hold the sword as if you were holding the tea cup. In fact, it is the same thing.'

The tea-ceremony master then went to face his adversary. He

told him, 'I have learned how to hold a sword, and am ready to die. You can now go ahead and kill me.'

With that he drew his sword and held it in readiness for the attack. The challenger observed the master's stance, and instead of lunging forward for the kill, he slowly lowered his weapon, saying, 'No, I withdraw the challenge. Your skill is evident. There is no way that I could kill you. I apologise for my rude behaviour.'

If you work physically every day, focusing on all the levels of awareness, clarity, and connectedness, the 'actor's body' will eventually become your natural state. Even if you are asked to do something completely new and unfamiliar, your body will respond appropriately. It will automatically find the easy and correct way of doing almost anything. L.M.

INTERIOR/EXTERIOR

Being able to constantly discover new ways to make your acting come alive requires great skill and awareness. In a sense, there are two elements in good acting: technical mastery, and the free and easy movement of the mind. In terms of your training, you work on developing and deepening both elements throughout your entire life.

When Yoshi uses the word 'mind' he is not referring to the brain or the intellect. There is a single word in Japanese, kokoro, which can be translated as either 'mind' or 'heart'. Probably, it is best to think about it as your 'inner self'. L.M.

You also use these two aspects of the actor's being every day as a part of your professional work. Both the mind and the technical mastery of the body are fully present when you perform. In this situation, they manifest themselves as inner and outer expression.

Balancing the interior movement with the exterior activity is a delicate business, but if skilfully done, it gives an unusual but interesting edge to your work. For example, the visible action on stage is very violent and passionate. If the inside is in the same state, the acting can appear too tense. So, you keep the interior very tranquil. If, on the contrary, you are portraying a calm or boring individual, and your interior is in the same state, there is a high risk that the performance will be extremely dull. In this case, your inside should work strongly with intense concentration and force. This will then support the calmness of the character or situation, while preventing it from becoming boring for the audience. Ideally, the interior and the exterior should be contradictory.

Look at a spinning top: when it wobbles about all over the place, it is spinning slowly. It is ready to fall over. When it is upright and fixed on a single spot, it is spinning extremely fast. On stage, your body is the same: when you are required to be calm or immobile, there is a huge inner dynamic. You 'spin' very fast inside. If this inner powerhouse is absent, quiet actions or moments of stillness have no impact.

The reverse is also true. When you undertake strong or violent physical actions, you must retain a core of tranquillity. Like the top, if you start to wobble about, you fall off your point of balance and cannot continue 'spinning'. Even when you are rampaging all over the stage, it should have a quality of effortlessness. This is a paradox; one aspect of the performance is calm, the other is dynamic. Actors need to experience this duality. When you discover physical stillness, it is not total stillness; there is also an inner dynamism. When you discover physical dynamism, you must balance it with inner calm.

What exactly is meant by 'inner calm'? It means that you are not the prisoner of turbulent emotions. Inside is empty; nothing bothers you. However, this 'calm' is not 'deadness' of feeling or a rigidly maintained state of unchanging 'tranquillity', but a fluid awareness that enables you to respond to shifts in the world around you.

If you are already gripped by a strong emotion, it is as if it is filling you up inside. There is no 'space' for any other sensation or feeling to enter. You are the prisoner of that feeling. For example, if you are overwhelmed by anger, it is impossible for any other emotion to spontaneously arise; nothing can change. So you need to throw away the anger in order to create some emptiness in your mind.

And once you have opened up that space, you have the freedom to react and respond to whatever comes along in the here and now.

In a sense, it is not feeling angry that is the problem, it is the fact that you have become trapped in the feeling of anger. Once the moment of genuine angry reaction has passed, let it go. The outside environment is constantly changing, and you need to be able to react to each moment as it comes toward you. As actors know, the minute you get emotionally stuck in a fixed state, your performance goes out the window.

Sometimes people get accustomed to a constant state of emotional turbulence. The emotions themselves may switch from joy, to sadness, to rage, but there is no moment of emptiness or calm in between. In this case, they have become addicted to the state of 'emotional intensity', which is just as rigid and limiting. L. M.

Balancing inside and outside. Moving without moving. Quiet but not quiet. Like riding a horse. A good rider can move very fast and cover a lot of ground, but he or she never seems agitated. The horse might be running across fields and ditches, through the forest, over the stream, and yet the rider remains tranquil and almost motionless. The actor's mind is the rider, the body is the horse.

A good rider consciously strives to unify him or herself with the horse, letting it move freely, while staying in control of every action. You give orders to the horse; you are the boss. The horse follows your will, but when you are riding well, the horse forgets about you, and you forget about the horse. The impulse of the horse and the impulse of the rider unify with each other until there is no division.

If however, you don't know how to ride, you will be working against the nature of the horse. You will be nervous and maybe a little apprehensive. Under these conditions there can be no calm, and the horse will become unsettled. There will be a struggle between you and the animal, until both of you become tired and irritable, and neither will manage to travel very far.

It is not enough to acquire a dynamic body (horse), and then acquire a calm but responsive mind (rider). You must also find ways to join them together, so that these two opposites work easily in relaxed harmony. L.M.

Zeami said, 'The body moves seven-tenths, the heart moves ten-tenths'.

When you are learning a role, you must do it one hundred per cent, using both the inner life and the physical expression to the maximum. However, if you continue to work the physical expression to the maximum when performing, you prevent the inner life from becoming accessible to the audience. If you slightly relax the outer expression, then what is happening inside can be felt by the audience. They will feel that they are watching something very interesting and involving.

However, we have to be careful how we use this idea of Zeami's, since it could lead to under-energised acting if wrongly applied. It does not mean that the outer form of expression becomes sloppy or less skilled, merely that the inner expression is given more emphasis in performance. In addition, if you have been rehearsing the external aspect of the role to the maximum extent prior to performance, the technique should be absolutely ingrained in the body. In which case, relaxing the exterior should be quite easy, and the performance will still be highly skilled. It will have the quality of technical 'ease' rather than effort, and will enable the audience to focus on the inner life.

Even when considering the external performance on its own, there is still a further need for contrast in expression.

Zeami suggested that if the body is working strongly with great force and energy, the legs should remain soft and delicate. If you are using the legs forcefully, the torso should remain calm and serene. If every part of the body is working equally strongly the acting can appear rough and crude. A strong performance should not lead to crude acting. An element of control and contrast in the use of the body creates a far more intriguing and polished performance.

REPETITION

In Japan, there is a Shinto tradition of walking in the mountains for a week with only a bit of brown rice as sustenance. Another tradition involves walking around a shrine one hundred times. It is believed that if you undertake and complete these actions, your prayers will be answered. The basis of these ceremonies is the act of repetition; it is the repeating that makes you change.

Although we often feel that daily life is repetitive, it is always slightly varied. We never really repeat in daily life. We wear different clothes, eat slightly different food, experience different moods. I am not saying that having an unchanging, monotonous life is good, but certain repeated actions can have a very strong effect. They can change you.

When you meditate, you sit in the same position, day after day. And in African dance, you move the pelvis (or sternum) forwards and backwards, creating a repeated pulse of the spine. The spine makes waves, and, if you continue this movement, your interior state alters. In the same way, the dervishes in the Middle East use constant turning to enter into a trance-like state. Every culture has a different version of doing these kind of exercises, but they all employ repetition. Why?

One way of thinking about this is to imagine that a human being has a kind of internal energy which exists alongside our physical energy. We nourish our physical aspect by watching what we eat, taking vitamins, getting enough sleep, and so on. But it is equally important to nourish our internal energy. Our inner sensitivity and awareness are as necessary for living as our physical well-being. It would seem that movement exercises that involve repetition some-how fulfil this function, and most cultures contain examples of such repeated physical activity. These exercises are usually found in the spiritual practices of the various traditions. But I suspect they are actually older than the religions in which they are found. The exercises were probably discovered by trial and error in order to stimulate inner energy. On seeing their effectiveness, various spiritual traditions decided to include these actions in their religious practice. In the same way, exercises involving repetition of sound are found in many religions, in the form of mantras or chants.

Over the centuries, we have forgotten the importance of feeding the inner senses, and so have lost contact with the physical activities that originally did this job. As a result, we can find inner exercises only within spiritual traditions, which have preserved and transmitted this knowledge. Nonetheless, everyone should 'feed' their internal energy, even if they are not a follower of a religious tradition. Repeated movements have the effect of stimulating your internal energy, making you more sensitive and aware as a person. In the past, Christian monks spent part of the day walking round and round the cloisters of the abbey, just as they do in Japanese Shinto shrines.

I have already mentioned the importance of the spine as a conduit for internal energy, and repeated movements involving the spine are especially useful. Even when the spine is not the focus of the action, the effect of repetition is very powerful.

This power has also been recognised in non-spiritual areas. I am reminded of the physical patterns used in regimented political movements such as Fascism. Followers of such political philosophies usually learn 'special' ways of moving (such as the 'goosestep' march) which involve an element of repetition. These movements are regularly practised, and this in turn confirms the individual's commitment to the group. In a sense, this kind of physical activity is very dangerous, since it serves to unify the followers into a single mass, focused only on a single shared goal.

Since the body and the mind are closely connected, rigid physical actions can promote a similar inflexibility of thinking. We must not assume that a tradition or philosophy that involves repeated movements is automatically wonderful. The difference lies in the fact that spiritual traditions use repetition in order to free the mind, while movements such as Fascism use it to fix the mind on a chosen objective.

Since your aim is to acquire freedom for the mind, be careful to choose exercises that avoid physical rigidity. Note that the classic upright 'Fascist' posture involves an extremely stiff body, as does the 'goosestep' movement.

Even in the martial arts, you must be careful to choose a good teacher, since the exercises are very powerful. If they are badly taught, they can become rigid or over-programmed, which can contribute to mental inflexibility. In the same way, when you do the exercises, you should work on keeping your concentration fluid and open, rather than tightly focused and narrow. The aim of all such training should be to encourage freedom of both body and mind, and anything that does the opposite should be avoided.

Repetition is a useful technique, but in real life we need to 'develop'. You can't just keep doing the same thing day after day after day: to maintain interest and to 'develop' yourself, you need to advance in some way. In a Zen monastery, you do the same thing each day at the same time. You sit in meditation, you work, you eat, you sleep. While this may be an effective form of spiritual training, actors are not monks. We need to work differently in order to change and grow.

One way to prevent repetition causing rigidity is to incorporate an element of contrast and variety into the work. In Shintoism they apply this idea through alternating periods of strong, dynamic activity with moments of calm. In fact, to be useful, all physical exercises should employ contrast.

When you alternate dynamic and gentle exercises the important factor is duration: how long you spend using one approach before shifting to the other. A good teacher will be able to judge just how long to continue a strong exercise before moving to a calmer one. This timing cannot be predicted. You cannot say that the dynamic work should last for twenty minutes, while the softer movements should take ten minutes. The correct duration of an exercise will depend on a number of factors, such as the day, the people, and the degree of experience. The teacher must be very sensitive to these factors when judging timings. If a teacher chooses well, the students feel affected by the exercise in a positive way; they might be tired, but they will also have a certain sense of exhilaration. When working on your own, if you feel that something has continued long enough, or that boredom is setting in, switch to another exercise.

However, it is sometimes interesting to deliberately keep the same exercise going, on and on and on. You might get bored, but at a certain point you may find that you have gone beyond boredom and broken through into another realm. You discover something completely new, something you have never encountered in ordinary life.

In our daily existence, we never break through the barrier of boredom. If something becomes too difficult or tedious, we simply stop doing it. Through being forced to stick with an exercise to the point of boredom and beyond, you have a chance to encounter a new space. And this helps your development.

In the daily life of ordinary Japanese people there is a great deal of repetition. You bow a lot. Your feeling towards other people is expressed in a clear physical movement: the more you respect a person the deeper your bow. Maybe this is why so many traditions have employed bowing as a mark of respect; it indicates and strengthens the connection between emotion and action.

Through doing these movements, you start to understand something that cannot be explained in logical terms. This is a kind of understanding that you don't find in a book, or through conversation: only through the body. Perhaps it is the understanding of what you are as a basic human being.

In many world religions, you sit for a long time, or you walk for a long time, and eventually you gain some kind of transcendent insight. What I find interesting about this is the way that the insight is assisted by some kind of physical activity. A good physical action is one that makes you change or enables you to understand better. And when you do the right kind of voice and movement exercises, you may find that your life feels happier, or your mind seems clearer, or your awareness becomes more sensitive. You somehow become stronger.

HUMAN ENERGY

A child splashes colours on a sheet of paper, producing a painting that is vibrant and colourful. It is beautiful, but that's all. Artists may use the same colours in an equally spontaneous way, yet somehow you get a different feeling when you look at their work, a strong sensation that seems to penetrate deep inside. It is just as beautiful as the child's painting, but it has an extra depth and resonance. Why does this happen? I feel that somehow the energy of the artist is transmitted to the onlooker via the colours, textures and shapes.

For an actor, the equivalent problem is maintaining a lot of 'presence' when you are faced with an audience. Although they may not put it into words, the audience can sense the performer's energy, and for them it is one of the main pleasures of theatre-going. Anything that increases your energy will help your acting.

When you see a good actor on the stage they look big: bigger than their actual physical reality. The same thing happens with attractiveness. Once, when I was younger, I watched an actress who looked incredibly beautiful on stage. I went to the stage door afterwards, and waited till she came out. But when she finally appeared, she was an ordinary looking woman, just like anyone else. Not the beautiful creature she had been while acting.

Stand firmly on the ground with your feet about a shoulder's width apart. Tilt your head backwards so that your face looks up into the sky. Open your mouth to the maximum. Open your eyes, nose and ears as far as you can. Stretch your arms above your head, and open the hands so that the palms are also facing the sky. Extend your tongue so that it pokes out of your mouth. In this position, with everything wide open and directed upwards toward the sky, make the sound 'Aaaah'. Keep going for as long as you can, and then gently bring the arms down, the head back to its normal position, and close the eyes and mouth. Just breathe quietly.

There are other similar exercises that help develop your human energy. As you get used to working in this way, you begin to notice exactly which elements bring you this energy. And you discover that the pleasure is not in 'getting energy', but rather the gradual understanding of the origin of that energy, and your relation to it. As you begin to sense the origin of this energy, it becomes less a matter of 'taking energy', and more a matter of 'unifying' yourself with that origin. You start to find real pleasure in this act of 'unification', and, as a consequence, even more energy arrives. And then your understanding deepens even further.

In Japanese Noh theatre the text is very archaic, dating from the thirteenth or fourteenth century, and it often uses the stylistic device of nature imagery. If a person is sad, they don't talk about what they are feeling, but they might say, 'Summer has gone. Winter will soon arrive. The autumn leaves are falling.' Emotion is described through the phenomena of nature.

What this tradition recognises is that the human being is a part of nature. Feeling sad or happy has an equivalent in the natural world, and human energy is linked to the energy of the physical environment. Today people imagine that they are independent of nature, and that what happens in the physical world has no influence on them. As a result, when you see the human being portrayed on stage, there is no connection to nature. But anyone who lives in an earthquake zone knows that we are very much part of the natural world. Not even the highest technology can protect you if the earth decides to shift.

In fact, human beings are totally connected to and dependent on nature. Air, water, fire, and even earth, are constantly moving, and we are a part of that motion. We should recognise this connection when we work in theatre. When we construct a human being on stage we should remember that he or she is linked to all the phenomena of nature. If we forget this, a whole dimension of what it is to be human is lost.

For example, I say the line 'I am angry!' If I think of myself as an isolated unit and focus only on my personal experience, the anger will be quite small. But if I think of the burning fire that roils in the core of the earth, the anger becomes much stronger and richer. Of course, the fire itself isn't 'angry'; rather my emotion has a counter-part in the natural world. In the same way, if I want to embody 'happiness', I can imagine that I am a part of the air circulating around me. In this way, the emotion doesn't simply happen inside me, it becomes a reflection of nature.

When we started working on *The Man Who*, Peter Brook called us together to explain that he wanted to make a theatre piece based on Oliver Sacks' book *The Man Who Mistook His Wife For A Hat*. We began the process by improvising certain scenes from the book. Up until this point, I had always thought that the subject matter for theatre had to be something that was directly connected with the experience of the audience. It might be about love, or family, or death, or politics, but it had to be something that the audience recognised from their own lives. But neurology? If it was psychology perhaps I could identify with it, since I might have experienced the same kind of emotional turmoil. But neurological damage is a very specific phenomenon, and is not often en-countered in most people's lives. So for me there was a problem with the material Peter had chosen to work on. I couldn't identify with it, and frankly, I wondered why on earth we were doing it.

Then people started improvising. I watched them, and suddenly I felt 'I am that person!' It was completely illogical, but I felt I was the same as that damaged individual. I was terrified. On a certain level, the scenes are really rather comical: a man who can't feel his left side looks a bit funny to watch. But I was terrified. It wasn't funny at all. That could be me up there, damaged but oblivious to the damage. There's no way to know. At that moment, I was surprised to realise how fully I could share in this project. In fact, since starting work with Peter Brook nearly thirty years ago, this turned out to be the best project for me.

Around that time, I was also thinking quite a lot about painting, especially representations of the human being. Before the invention of the camera, one of the main functions of portraiture was to record personalities and events. That isn't needed any more, since photographs do the same job. Instead, modern artists who paint the human form are using it to say something about how they see people. It is a personal view of human beings that is being communicated. So I decided to do the same sort of thing with my acting: present my own way of looking at the human being. However, I wasn't sure how to do this in practice.

When we began rehearsals, we didn't know which style we would use to perform this piece. We decided that the first step was to find out as much as possible about the neurological problems themselves, and so for four months we visited the Salpêtrière neurological hospital in Paris to meet and talk with patients. We read case studies and reports sent from England. We got more information from Oliver Sacks. We watched television documentaries.

When we were doing the observation in the hospital, certain things struck me very forcefully. There was one patient who was struggling to emerge from a coma. There was another who had only two weeks to live. What I saw in those patients was how strong the basic human energy is. The kind of energy that was pushing the body to come out of coma. The energy to continue living when the body is so close to death. The coma patient was obviously not conscious, yet something inside him was driving the body to wake up. This kind of human energy is incredibly strong. It doesn't matter whether the person is immobile, or near to death, something keeps fighting to maintain life.

I realised that in comparison to this energy, being paralysed on the left side is only a surface detail. Of course, being paralysed still matters, but in comparison to this ferocious urge to continue living, it is only a detail. This energy was astonishing to see. It was also very beautiful.

There was another patient who could not move at all, except that when somebody played music, he could dance. I realised that the human being is a mystery. Neurologists can give an explanation for this and other phenomena, but I still feel that there is something very mysterious about the human being. Even the body is a mystery. You cannot fully explain it.

So when I was performing in *The Man Who* I decided I would try to convey how beautiful the human being is, and how mysterious. As a consequence, when working on my various roles in the play, I didn't worry about portraying specific characters. Neurological problems and the basic human energy are not linked to any personal situation. I simply concentrated on building the scenes detail by detail, action by action. And little by little, a human being emerged. I found this process interesting. At the same time, I tried to use the minimum number of actions needed to convey the reality of that character's situation. Too much detail would have obscured the inner reality. We would not have been able to see the incredible beauty of the essential human being.

SELF-OBSERVATION

When exploring movement, try to include research on actions that are totally symmetrical. They make you really think about what you are doing with your body. The human form has a centre line running down the middle, with one eye, one nostril, one ear, one arm, and one leg placed on each side of the body. It is as if the right side is a mirror image of the left. However, we rarely have a conscious awareness of this fundamental structure, and our actions are seldom truly symmetrical. To experience this kind of movement, try moving the right and left sides of the body to equal degrees and at the same moment. For example, you raise both arms, or you open both eyes to the maximum, or you twist both feet inwards. It doesn't matter what you do, or how it looks; it's just nice to discover all the possibilities of symmetry, and to see how that feels inside.

It is extremely difficult to verify your own work. When you are practising your various exercises, ask another person to observe what you are doing. For example, when you attempt to place your body in a specific position (e.g. with the arms absolutely parallel to the earth), you might be slightly out. Ask someone to correct you, since it is important to learn how to be perfectly accurate and precise in whatever you do. Once you have learnt where the true horizontal position for your arms lies, you keep practising it so that your body can eventually move there easily and automatically. But you need to find where the correct position is situated before you can go there with confidence. In the same way, get someone to listen to your voice and speech, to check for accuracy. If you get someone to help you from the beginning of your training, you will learn to do the exercises correctly without needing to check each time.

By the way, it is best to ask other people for help in this area, since mirrors, tape recorders and videos are not true 'reflections' of what you are doing.

This kind of checking is only to be employed in the early stages of learning. In performance, you cannot 'look to see' whether you are doing a movement correctly or not. You must be able to position your body by feel alone. As a performer, you must know exactly where your body is at all times, and every move should be chosen, not accidental.

A lot of actors don't like to be criticised. When I am working on a project, I might say something to another performer, who then becomes angry. I have observed this pattern on many occasions, whether or not I am the one who makes the comment. Maybe the actor is right to feel upset. Maybe it is wrong to criticise, since if you say too much you can end up confusing an actor.

From my own point of view, I like to listen to whatever criticism is offered. For me, the basic problem remains that I can't watch myself in action. Even a video recording doesn't help, since it can't reflect all the detail and nuances of the live performance. You can't act in front of a mirror. It isn't a 'true reflection'. So the comments other people make are useful; they fulfil the function of a mirror. But a critic (of any kind, including any of your fellow actors) is like a distorting mirror which already carries its own shape and direction. If you believe what it 'reflects' too literally, you can come away with a false impression. A critic's words are not a true reflection of what you are doing. You must allow for distortion.

Nonetheless all information is useful. It doesn't matter if you don't listen to everything, or follow all the suggestions exactly. I find that other people's perceptions are valuable, and so I want to get as many of them as possible. Sometimes, friends say that I listen too much to other people. They suggest that maybe I lack confidence. This might be true, but it isn't the reason I like to listen to criticism. I don't feel obliged to follow every comment, but, through what people say, I can get information about my work, and this helps me see what is actually happening. Even a distorted mirror is better than no mirror at all. Comments might not be 'true', but they are useful.

A Kabuki actor once said, 'If you think that someone is a better actor than you, he is far, far superior. If you think that you are both about the same, he is distinctly better than you. If you feel he is inferior, then the two of you are actually the same standard.'

In fact, the audience is the true mirror. I don't really know how to act my part until I get in front of the audience. At that moment I discover my role. The rehearsal room is just the preparation that enables the discovery. The audience tells me how to play.

I believe that the actor's job is not to show what he or she can do, but to bring the audience into another time and space. A place that the audience does not encounter in daily life. The actor is like the driver of the car that transports the audience somewhere else, somewhere extraordinary. I want to serve the audience in this way.

When you act, you are totally involved with the character you are playing. If the character is sad, your body and emotions move accordingly. At the same time, there is another 'you' who is ordering the performance, who is not at all sad. You can feel the relationship between the 'you' who is fully engaged in the moment, and the 'you' that stands outside and watches.

The 'watcher' gives the orders; for example, it decides to initiate a change in body shape that in turn alters the feelings. This process is very interesting to observe, and you are aware of your 'self' watching your other 'self'. At the same time, you don't really know how the relationship between the body and the emotions operates. You initiate an emotional shift by altering the body, something changes, you watch it happen, but you don't understand why it works. And then you start searching for another 'you', who is making this happen.

As an exercise, try to perform a character, using only one part of the body. For example, you play the role of Hamlet, in its full complexity, using only one hand. Then you try using the other hand to give life to the character of Ophelia. It is like puppetry, except that the puppet is a part of your own body. When you do this, you are acting via the manipulation of your hand. Then do exactly the same thing using your whole body instead of just your hand. You simply manipulate your whole body in the same way that you manipulated your hand.

As an actor, you watch and manipulate your body, and as a consequence of your manipulation, something changes, and a new emotion comes to you. Yet at the same time, you watch this new emotion emerge, almost as if it is something unfamiliar and surprising. But who is this person who is watching?

This is a story from China. Once upon a time there was a rich man who had four wives. The first wife was extremely beautiful, and he took her everywhere with him, and proudly displayed her to everyone he met. Whatever she asked for he bought her: jewels, fine silks, rare delicacies. He always bathed with her, and would humbly wash her from head to foot. Eventually she became extremely vain and conceited, and started ordering her husband about.

The second wife had been acquired after a lot of struggle. He had worked hard, negotiated, and fought to gain this bride, for the marriage had consolidated his position in the community. He loved her very much, and was pleased with this second marriage since it brought him a sense of security. Although he felt less real love towards this new wife (since he had been forced to work so hard to gain her), he swore he would do anything for her. He told her that he was willing to become a cheat, a murderer, or whatever was necessary to ensure that she stayed with him.

His third wife was not particularly important to him. He felt mild affection towards her, since when he had first married her, she had been young and attractive. She had accompanied him on his frequent travels, mainly so that he could continue to enjoy a sexual relationship when away from home. But as time went on, he started to see her weaknesses and faults. He remembered that in the beginning it had been different, and this led to shouting and quarrels. He called her 'stupid', 'insensitive', 'ill-educated' and 'idiotic'. They nearly divorced, but when she suddenly presented her husband with a baby, he decided to continue with the marriage.

The fourth wife was treated like a servant. The husband ordered her about, beat her, and never gave her any type of gift or praise. Not even kind words. The poor woman was in great despair, since her husband loved her so little. Eventually she became weak and depressed, constantly worrying about her behaviour, and desperately trying to please her husband. She scuttled around the house, flinching in fear of yet another harsh word or blow.

One day the Government asked the man to undertake a long journey beyond the frontier of the empire. Since by now he was quite old, he didn't want to travel on his own, and decided to ask one of his wives to accompany him. He loved the first wife the most, and so went to her with his request. When he asked her to come on the journey, she just looked coldly at him, then replied, 'No. Never, never, never.'

With those words she turned her back on him. The husband was very angry, but nothing he said would move her. So he went to the second wife, and made the same request. Her expression didn't alter as she continued brushing her hair. She responded with a single word: 'No.'

He was shocked by her heartlessness, and decided to approach the third wife. She was the one who organised the day-to-day running of the household, and looked after him when he was ill, so he felt she would be well qualified to care for him on this long and arduous journey. When he asked her to accompany him, she burst into tears, saying, 'I really want to go with you, but I must stay and look after the baby. Also, I am scared of going somewhere so unfamiliar. In fact I'm terrified. I'll go with you as far as the border, but after that, please forgive me, I can't go any further.'

He agreed to this and went off in search of his fourth wife. Since he hadn't treated her at all well, he was rather doubtful about her reply. But she said her job was to stay by the side of her husband, and stated that she was ready to go anywhere with him, even into Hell itself. The man was both surprised and touched by her willingness to accompany him.

The day of departure arrived. The first wife stayed in bed, refusing to speak or even alter the coldness of her expression. The second wife reacted in the same way, saying nothing, not even wishing him goodbye. The third wife was busy organising all the details of the journey. She kept her word and travelled as far as the frontier. When they arrived there, she wept, kissed her husband, then turned returned home. The man travelled on into this strange foreign country, accompanied only by his fourth wife.

So what are these four 'wives'? The first one is the body, the second is possessions, the third is your spouse, or relationships with people. And the fourth? It is your real self. The frontier is death;

your body and possessions will not travel with you. Your husband or wife can go only as far as the border. The only one that stays with you is the one you have so badly abused: yourself.

We tend to think about our bodies as if they are our 'self'. It is true, you can use your body, but it is not your property. The only thing you really 'own' is your mind and inner being.

Look at a flower; the first thing you see are the delicate petals. But if you look behind the blossom, you can see the woody stem. The fragile beauty is real, but something else supports it. This is true of everything; there is a surface that you can see, but there is always 'something else' behind. Even a huge mountain will have streams of water flowing underneath.

With human beings, there is a visible surface with a great deal lurking inside. What you see is supported by what you cannot see. For this reason, you must not make the mistake of training only what is visible on the surface. It simply doesn't work. If you want to have a beautiful flower, you have to concentrate on watering the roots of the plant, and supporting the stem as it grows. In the same way, if you want to have a beautiful body and stage presence, you have to take care of your inner self. If the inside is poorly nourished, no amount of beautiful gesturing, extraordinary vocal technique, elegant costumes, or fancy makeup will help. Without the inside, it just doesn't work.

I can ask the question: 'What is water?'

You might reply by giving examples such as, 'the sea, a river, what comes out of the tap,' but these aren't 'water'. They are the 'forms' in which 'water' appears. In a sense there is no such thing as 'water' on its own. No fundamental form for 'water' itself.

When we see 'water' it is contained in some 'shape' or another. A bucket, an ocean, a drop of rain. If water is put into a round cup, it takes the shape of the cup, and its movement is constrained by that form. If it appears in a river it follows the course of the riverbed, and as the landscape changes, with narrowing gorges or sudden descents, the force and speed of the water alters as well. In a lake it takes a complex shape with inlets and islands, and under the influence of the sun's heat, it can transform into vapour. Water has hundreds of 'shapes', but whatever the shape we can always recognise 'water'. L.M.

Humans are the same. Just as we know that 'water' exists, even though we can only see it when it takes the form of its 'container', the 'human being' exists beyond the 'shapes' we see.

Even a single person has many 'shapes'. Sometimes our shape comes from what we do: we are a student, or a philosopher, or a labourer. These are our costumes. Or we are shaped by age and changing responsibilities: a child, a parent, an old person. A single individual may appear in several 'forms' within the space of an evening, changing from 'tough-minded boss' to 'sympathetic friend' to 'responsible parent' to 'silly, romantic lover'. All of these roles are true, but they are not complete. They are simply the 'shapes' in which the essential human being appears. L.M.

A Zen master once described the body as a mass of red flesh which the real human being continually enters and exits. Many people assume that the body they see is the totality of their self. While this mass of red flesh is certainly a human being, inside the body another kind of 'human being' exists; something independent of the conglomeration of blood and tissue. This other self is free and constantly changing. It is your real self.

When you are acting, the aim is not to show the 'character' you are playing. Beyond the character a more fundamental human being exists, and it is this 'fundamental human being' that makes the stage come alive. Simply constructing 'the character' isn't enough.

BODY AND EMOTIONS

The actor tries to look 'natural' on stage. This is true of all styles of theatre. Even an actor playing in a stylized production aims to appear natural on stage. By 'natural', I mean 'human': something 'real' is generated by the actor and is felt by the audience.

Sometimes you discover this 'natural' acting through a deep

psychological investigation. And you may produce something that is truly 'natural' and organically human. But it doesn't always work, since the emotional path of investigation is difficult, and occasionally elusive. An actor requires methods which will produce a believable 'human' performance every single night, irrespective of what the actor is actually feeling.

We know that the mind, the body, and the emotions are inextricably linked to each other. When you are sad, your shoulders cave in, your head drops forward, your thoughts become pessimistic, and you feel that nothing is going right for you in your life. When you are happy, the body opens out, the chest expands, the head lifts, and somehow you feel that everything you hope for is possible. Your body position, your thoughts, and your emotions always change together.

As actors, we usually start our work from the mind or emotions, and then assume that this inner life will travel outwards and appear through our bodies. But the opposite method also works: starting from the outside and then moving inwards.

You can use laughter to explore this idea. Make the sound 'Ha, ha, ha, ha, ha.' Do it in a loud voice. Don't worry about whether or not you feel amused, just do it. Whenever a large group does this together, everyone always ends up collapsing in genuine laughter. It becomes natural.

As an actor, it is quite difficult to generate spontaneous-sounding laughter. Even if you try to recall hilarious moments in your experience, it very rarely works. This is because it is usually extremely hard to change your emotional state by willpower alone. You can try telling yourself to feel happy or sad, but the self doesn't usually listen. But if you change what the body is doing, it starts to affect your emotions, and this makes it easier to produce believable acting. Also, in real life you never decide to laugh, it simply happens. You never think: 'What is there in my past that was funny?' You just laugh. If you think about it, it is too late, the moment is past. Laughter is spontaneous and it is not easy to deliver spontaneity on demand.

However, there are two things that you need to remember if you
are constructing a performance from the outside. Firstly, as I
mentioned before, a performance always involves full engagement
and concentration. The actor can concentrate on either the interior
feeling (if working from the inside to the outside), or the physical
action (if working from the outside to the inside), but the
concentration must be there. Something is always happening
inside. You can't just construct the outside, and then forget about
it. Secondly, the external form that the actor is using must be based
on human reality. You can't just use any movement pattern and
hope that it will work. You must use a pattern that is natural and
accurate.

I once saw a performance of a Noh play called *Fujito* which really
affected me. In it, the actor had to portray an old woman, filled with
grief over the death of her son.

*The actor playing the old woman was a man. In both the traditional
Noh theatre and Kabuki, all the roles are performed by men. There are no
women on stage. In Noh, the actor will wear a female mask, and incarnate
the essence of that woman character. In Kabuki, the actor wears heavy
makeup, a wig, and elaborate costume in order to present a skilled and
elegant portrayal: an idealised vision of femininity. L.M.*

This old woman decided to confront her son's murderer. She
slowly walked from the wings along the 'bridge' that led to the stage
where the murderer was waiting. As the actor walked, I really felt
all the grief, anger, despair, and determination of that old woman.
I went backstage afterwards, wanting to understand how he had
been able to bring this extremely complex character to life. I asked
him what he had been thinking or feeling before he entered the
stage. The actor responded, 'This is an old woman, so when I walk
I must concentrate on making the steps a little shorter than usual.
And I must stop at the first pine tree.'

*In the Noh theatre, the bridge that links the wings to the stage is fully
visible to the audience, and has three small pine trees spaced along its
length L.M.*

In the West, the actor might try to fill himself with feelings of sadness, anger or whatever before stepping onstage. But in the case of this Noh actor, there was no effort to create an interior life; yet somehow the old woman was fully believable. Although he claimed he was simply following the 'choreography', I suspect that he was subconsciously in contact with the feelings involved in that scene. The important thing was that he did not try to make them personal. He did not go into details. Noh theatre is about universal experiences, not personal responses. The experience of that old woman had to suggest the totality of all human desolation and loneliness, not merely one individual's problems. Because of this, Noh demands a different level of engagement than most Western theatre. In this performance, the actor was concentrating everything on precisely what he had to do with his body. He gave all of himself to the task, and remained totally in the moment.

Here is an exercise, using two short pieces of text, which are:

'I don't have any money. I have no food. I am hungry.'

And:

'Maybe tomorrow I'll have some money. I can buy food. I can eat all I want.'

Usually, if given these lines, you would think about how to speak them. Maybe do the first phrase in a dark or low voice. Maybe slowly. The second phrase with more vocal energy, or louder. This is the normal way, but it is interesting to try another path, which uses the connection between body and emotion.

When speaking the first phrase, try to find an appropriate body position, maybe hunched over, or collapsed. Something that feels absolutely right for what you are saying. Then fix that body shape in your mind. Then find a new body shape that fits the second phrase. Maybe standing taller, or with a more open shape. Remember this position.

Now take the first body position again, really taste that shape, and then say the phrase. Move into the second position, while observing the path of the transformation. Don't just step out of position A, and then construct position B. Feel how the body needs to move to get you from A to B, and how the inner dynamic shifts at the same time. When you arrive at position B, say the second phrase.

The next stage is to do the exercise with just a tiny movement of the body, something that an onlooker wouldn't notice: for example, letting only the sternum (breastbone) go from A to B. You have already observed how the inner dimension shifted as the body altered position. Remember how the interior transformation happened. Now say the lines while maintaining the inner movement from position A to position B. Nothing happens on the outside. Just the lines.

The inside is not changing because of the text. The body remembers the physical journey and the inner dynamic shift. The text follows.

In the play *The Man Who*, I had the role of a patient who had lost the ability to perceive the left side of his body. In one scene he was requested by the doctors to carefully shave his entire face in front of a mirror. So he did. But since he had no awareness of his left side, he shaved only the right half of his face. He was absolutely convinced that he had shaved it all. Meanwhile he was being recorded on video. The doctors then asked him to turn and look at himself in the video monitor. Whilst, in the mirror reflection, the patient's left side appeared on his left, on the video screen it appeared to him on his right, and he could see that half of his face was still covered in shaving foam. At that moment he understood that his brain was damaged.

In terms of staging, I had to look at the video screen and then back at the mirror three times, in order to compare the two images of my face. Each repeated turn of the head had to develop the situation. The first time the man turned was when the doctor asked him to look at the video screen. So I simply swivelled my head. The second time, the man couldn't comprehend what he had seen, so he had to verify the image on the screen. The third time was desperation. Three steps. In order to give the appropriate development, I changed the tempo each time I turned my head. It sounds mechanical, but each time I actually performed it, I found that I genuinely felt sadness. I don't know why. I wasn't looking for the emotion. But because of the tempo and the interior connection, I discovered I had tears running down my face.

In fact, the whole of my performance was constructed through tiny physical details. Turn to the screen at 'this' tempo. Next time stop a little bit on the way. Tilt the head very slightly to the right. And the emotion emerged.

As an actor, if I look for emotion first, I tend to panic. I think, 'Yesterday, I felt genuinely sad. So today I must find that same sadness again.'

But when I try to think 'I am feeling sad', sadness never comes.

It is extremely difficult to repeat the same emotion over and over again. You are taking a big risk when you depend on your emotions as the basis for reproducing a scene when you have a long run. On the other hand, you can repeat body details in exactly the same way every day. Working from body shape is useful for actors.

In Japanese classical theatre, the performance is totally constructed from the outside. The actor learns the movements of the play as if it is a piece of dance choreography. Every step, turn of the head, and emotional gesture is fixed by tradition. Even the exact vocal intonations are prescribed, and must be learned as part of the script. These physical and vocal forms are called kata.

There is no improvisation; a young actor copies his master exactly, in order to learn the kata *of any given role. Once these have been perfectly mastered (and only then) might an actor be permitted to give the performance a 'personal touch'. But this would only be a matter of nuance, or subtle shading of the existing* kata, *not the creation of an entirely new interpretation. L. M.*

Noh plays are usually divided into two sections. There is a short 'interval' between the acts, which gives the main performer the time to go into the wings and change his costume. During this 'interval', a comic Kyogen actor often comes on stage and explains the entire story to the audience. One day, a very fine Noh actor listened while he was getting changed, and said, 'Ah! So *that's* what this play is all about!'

It was the first time he had heard the whole story. Although he had learned his part perfectly and could give a fantastic performance, he didn't have a clue about what was supposed to happen next. He had created the role from the outside, following the kata laid down by tradition. Yet despite this, the audience was still moved by the performance and could feel the entire reality of the story.

In Peter Brook's production of the *Mahabharata*, I played a character called Drona, a master warrior who could not be beaten in combat. In the play, Drona's enemies were desperate to eliminate him before the climactic battle, since if he participated they would be faced with certain defeat. So they cheated. In order to make Drona lose the will to fight, they lied and told him his son had been killed. The trick succeeded. In despair at losing his son, Drona committed suicide.

In the suicide scene, Drona took off his outer garments, and then poured a large jar of blood-red water over his head, as a kind of purification. The liquid ran down his entire body and then soaked into the earth. The audience felt the grief, love, and despair of the father very strongly. But for myself, I didn't think, 'What should appear in this moment?' or 'What psychological state should I use?'

As the scene started, Toshi Tsuchitori (the Japanese musician who was involved in the production) began a steady drum beat. I used this as my focus, and simply concentrated on relating my movements to the beat of the drum. For me, there was nothing else. Only the link between the sound and the actions of my body. Of course, I remained aware of Jo, Ha, Kyu, and I remembered the nature of the situation. It was a bleak moment, not a cheerful one, so I retained awareness of the sad quality of the scene. I didn't play 'the sadness'. It was simply acknowledged as being present. For me the work was to create a relationship with the drum, while developing Jo, Ha, Kyu.

On reflection, I suspect that this moment worked because I had been so firmly concentrated on one single thing. As a consequence, there was a lot of space 'inside' me; space which allowed the audience's imagination to enter. I didn't fill my interior with too much psychological material. I simply respected the situation, and then concentrated on the music. In turn, this concentration created a kind of inner void. Into this emptiness the audience could project their own imagination. They could make up all sorts of stories about what I was feeling.

The empty space of theatre exists inside the actor, as well as on the stage itself. My Noh teacher once said that you must not perform theatre 'in your own way'. Instead you should try to do exactly what your teacher shows you. The way of raising the hand, the manner of speaking the lines, everything must be done exactly as he says. Even if you think it is incorrect. You must not alter or re-interpret what you have learned until you are sixty years old. Then you can be free. But since you begin Noh training at the age of five or six, we are actually talking about more than fifty years of study. At this point, you have fully assimilated your style, and so even if you improvise or adapt the work, you will never betray it. Everything that you have learned in the previous fifty years provides a firm base, which in turn enables you to know what real freedom is.

I met my master years after he had told me this, when he was about seventy-five years old. I asked him if he still felt the same now that he had attained the 'age of freedom'. He replied, 'No. What I told you applies only to geniuses. I am an ordinary actor, and cannot achieve freedom. Quite the reverse, in fact. I have absolutely no freedom now. I am getting old and I sometimes find that I go blank, or forget the lines. I become so worried about forgetting the lines that I have no time to concentrate on finding freedom. My main concern is simply to do the job correctly. That's all.'

A few years ago I went to see a performance given by a brilliant Japanese actor called Hisao Kanze, who has since died. Many critics have suggested that it was the quality of his work that encouraged a whole younger generation to become interested in Noh theatre. One thing I noticed about his performance was that the storyline was extremely clear. This was probably one of the reasons why he was so popular with a young audience. Unfortunately, for me it was a little disappointing. His performance was excellent, but when the entire story was so clearly told, I felt it was rather like watching a melodrama on television. Then he came to Paris and presented the same play. It was absolutely wonderful.

I went backstage afterwards to talk to him. He explained that when he performed in Japan, he concentrated on the story and the dramatic situation. Since the language used in the Noh theatre is extremely archaic, most Japanese have difficulty understanding the exact meaning of the text. He therefore felt that it was important to bring clarity to the action.

In Europe, there was no possibility of the audience following the lines, so he had a different aim. Instead of trying to tell the story very clearly, he focused on each gesture, on each sound, on each detail of every moment. It was riveting to watch, and managed to have an emotional impact despite the unintelligibility of the story.

A French critic saw this performance and noted what happened to her. At first she was just sitting and watching in a relaxed way, but gradually she found herself starting to straighten up, and her spine took a more poised position (as in the meditation position). Although she couldn't understand the action, she felt something very powerful coming from the stage.

I think the fact that Kanze was no longer worrying about telling the story in terms of emotion, meaning, or psychology, enabled him to reach another level of performance. The need to concentrate on each moment with his entire being rather than worrying about getting the text across, had forced him away from the conventional kind of theatrical storytelling. He had managed to find a more universal level of communication – human being to human being – that even a non-Japanese critic could sense.

However, there can be a problem with the traditional approach. If you only work on the outside, it feels very artificial. Nothing comes out of your performance. It is empty.

If you are too careful about the externals of your performance – your gestures, your costume, your makeup, your expression – the inner dimension will be bland. It is as if you have constructed a beautiful 'box' but inside the 'box' there is nothing. It is empty. The audience won't be moved, since the 'box' contains nothing of interest. If, however, I concentrate only on the internal performance, I have another problem. Since there is no structure or technique (the 'box') to contain my inner life, you can't see anything. It's just messy and boring. You need to construct an interesting 'box', and then ensure that it is filled with something equally interesting.

The 'emptiness' that Yoshi is referring to here is the absence of inner life. The 'positive emptiness' that he has spoken of on earlier pages is different; it is a state full of inner engagement, the kind of 'emptiness' where the audience senses that the actor is totally present, and that anything could happen. This is the kind of 'emptiness' that can be used to 'fill the box'. L .M.

In real life, it is impossible isolate your mental habits. Since the mind has no tangible reality, you cannot grapple with it in order to change your way of thinking, or your world-view. In the same way, trying to ignore a strong emotion (such as anger or despair), or to diminish its importance, is very difficult. These are things that don't change easily. But the body can be altered quite directly. We can see it, we can touch it, it has a tangible reality that our emotions and thoughts don't have. And since our body is connected to the other aspects of ourselves, changing our bodies can change the rest. Next time you find yourself hunched over in despair, start moving your body, paying particular attention to freeing the spine and expanding the chest and shoulder region. Open out, look upwards and all around, breathe strongly and deeply, relax the neck, and find a positive image to stimulate your movements. You should find that your mood starts to lift, and that your thoughts stop running in the same tiny circles.

Working with the body is not something that actors do simply for health, or to improve their performance. If you get into the habit of regularly exploring your body so that it becomes very free and responsive, your mental processes become equally flexible. In addition, your emotional life will become richer.

Details

I was working with some students on *Waiting for Godot* by Beckett. In this, the character Lucky speaks a long, boring monologue. As the student was doing this speech, I interrupted him and asked, 'What are you looking for?'

The student replied, 'I am looking for the boringness.'

As an actor, you cannot act philosophy, or an idea or a state. It's impossible. A director might say to you, 'At this moment your existence is frozen, you have no energy, you are cut off from society. Speak it.' But you cannot act this situation. The actor can speak very concrete things: perhaps whispering, discovering each word one by one. Afterwards the audience might come up with their own interpretation, such as, 'That man has lost himself.' That is fine, but the actor cannot play 'lost himself'.

Moreover, if you are trying to convey 'boring', you must play a very interesting version of 'boring'. If the audience feels you are making them yawn, this isn't 'boring' in the theatre, it is real-life boring. As an actor, you can't speak the lines in a 'boring' way, or else the audience will fall asleep.

Instead of playing a state, you look for very concrete details. Once these have been assembled, the audience can get a sense of 'who you are'. In daily life, you do not 'play the character' of 'your-self'. One minute you do *this* action, then immediately you do *that* action, and then *another* action. Afterwards, you can look at what you did and recognise what kind of character you are, but you don't decide to do *this* action because your character 'demands' it. And maybe tomorrow you will do something totally different. It isn't a case of 'because my character is like *this*, I have to do *that* next.' Never. At each moment you choose one action, one word, one phrase.

When you are preparing a role, it is very easy to broadly characterise the person you are playing, to say, 'He is a cynic,' or, 'She is optimistic.' But how can you play a person this way? You can't play a description. What you can do is find a lot of small details. At this moment his head lifts. At that moment her voice becomes stronger. And as these details accumulate, the audience will get an impression of the individual. They will eventually decide that the character is cynical or optimistic. Start with the development of small details.

However, there are a couple of notes of caution for this kind of work. Firstly, you must be sure that you have discovered the correct details. Secondly, your body movements and your inner dynamic must be firmly linked. You have to spend a lot of time searching for the exact 'right' detail for each dramatic moment. And you can only do this when you already have a very strong sense of connection between your body and the inner dimension.

When your body is well linked to your interior being, the smallest physical changes evoke distinct inner sensations. You can sense what the difference is between standing with your forefinger curled into your palm, and holding it straight. And you are clear about which feelings are linked to the various details. You can sense that having the thumb in *this* position evokes a sense of assertive-ness, whereas in *that* position, you feel more reticent.

In order to create a role using this approach, you need to spend time experimenting with a range of physical possibilities. You also have to be very exact and honest about what you feel. It is no good finding the body position that feels 'sort of' correct. You must find the precise physical detail that is clearly and strongly linked to the emotion of the moment. Once you have found all the essential shapes, you can link them to form a kind of 'map' of the emotional journey. Then you simply follow the physical 'map' each time you perform. But you need to take the time to find the right details, in order to create the right 'map'.

When you are doing your research to find the physical details, you can sometimes conduct your experiments 'in miniature'. For example, the move you may need to find is a jump, but this can be quite hard (and tiring) to explore. So you start by concentrating on the movements of one hand. As already noted in the section on 'tasting' (page 28), your hand has a lot of possibilities: five fingers, the palm, different angles, clenched, relaxed. So you play around with it. At a certain moment you feel joy and your hand suddenly opens. This is the right feeling, the one you need, and the movement is strongly connected to it. However, on stage I will need a bigger description, so I enlarge the action of 'suddenly opening my hand' into a jump. But getting to the 'jump' is a delicate process.

I start from one hand. The correct feeling there. Then I allow the whole of the body to become the same as that one hand. (In fact, using the hand isn't really a 'miniature version'; the whole of the feeling is there. Only sometimes the entire body becomes the hand.) As an actor, you decide how big you want to make that 'hand'; it can stay small, or involve the whole physique. In a sense, it doesn't really matter how big the movement is. What matters is finding the body movement that corresponds to the interior movement. Once you have found this, the scale is a matter of choice. You can start small and then enlarge the pattern, or you can start big and then reduce its size.

We can look at some general physical acting exercises. First, soften the face into a kind of neutral expression: all the muscles are relaxed (including the mouth and eyes), and it appears calm and unemotional. Try to keep it in this state, while you move the rest of the body. Try to explore all the physical possibilities of all the muscles, and as you do it, 'taste' what is happening (see page 28). In this way, you can really sense the body function and its effect.

Then do the opposite. Sculpt the face into a kind of extreme expressive mask, while keeping the body calm. You will soon find that the body wants to respond to what is suggested by the face. Take the exercise one step further, and permit the body to shape itself in sympathy with the face. Make sure that this is an instinctive response, not a case of the brain deciding, 'Oh, I have an angry expression on my face, so I think I will raise my arm and clench my fist.' Instead, the body senses what the expression is offering, and unifies itself with the face. Once this unity has been established, you try to sense what voice belongs to this being; starting by using sounds (rather than words) to find the voice. You have now created a kind of living sculpture, using the face, then the body, and finally the voice. Now that sculpture starts to move, and eventually interacts with other characters.

Now the other way round. Rather than starting with the movement and then finding the inner connection, you can hold a specific image in your mind, and then let it carry your body into movement. You are giving your body permission to move freely, led by an image. However, for this exercise to be really effective, you need to have a strong and rich imagination, to enable your body to move in many ways and not get stuck in stereotyped patterns.

It is also nice to use ideas that relate to the essence of human experience, rather than superficial or distant images. For example, imagine you are living inside your mother's womb, moving on your journey towards birth. For this, you have to search for who you are before you have joined the outside world. Or, make visible, through movement, the horrible aspects of your own character. In a sense, exploring these potent images also acts as a kind of self-therapy, helping you to cleanse you inside.

Your imagination can subtly affect your body even where there is no movement or physical contact. Think about a colour such as red or yellow. Really concentrate, and unify your whole being with that colour without trying to demonstrate it on the outside. Your whole existence becomes red. Then ask the onlookers to guess which colour you are using. Of course, it doesn't work all the time, but in a high proportion of cases the audience will choose the correct colour. This means that if you have a strong imagination, the audience can sense what is happening. It isn't necessary to 'demonstrate'. Communication occurs when you fully unify yourself with your intention. Your imagination will subtly alter your being and your actions, and the audience can feel it. They will understand.

Tai and yu

When Yoshi describes building a performance through the accumulation of surface details, he is not insisting that this is the only way. Sometimes you work from the outside to the inside. Sometimes the other way round. L.M.

One of Zeami's more difficult but useful ideas was the division of learning into 'fundamental structure' and 'phenomenon'. In Noh theatre, these are called *tai* and *yu*. In poetic terms, *tai* is the flower, while *yu* is the scent; *tai* is the moon, while *yu* is the moonlight. If, when you study acting, you concentrate on the fundamental structure – the inside – the 'phenomenon' – the outside expression – will emerge automatically. Very often, actors will see an 'effect' and decide to imitate it, but this will not produce good acting. Instead, you need to understand where that 'effect' originates, and what causes it to come into being. If you copy the outside expression of something without understanding its fundamental structure, your work will have no meaning.

For example, if you are playing the part of an old man or woman, you must understand what age actually does to the mind and body, and how each character ages in a unique way according to his or her experience of life and the individual personality. Too often you see generalised 'doddering' rather than a real and truthful depiction of a particular person at a particular age. If you try to show age by copying the outside 'phenomenon' of, say trembling hands, rather than understanding the 'fundamental structure' of emotional effort coming through an enfeebled body, you will only produce a cliché. L.M.

In dealing with the concepts of *tai* and *yu*, it is important to remember that *both* are equally necessary in a performing situation. If you have no fundamental structure behind your action, the details of expression cannot arise in any kind of truthful fashion; but equally, if you don't know how to let this deep structure become visible to the audience, no communication can take place.

Returning to the example of portraying an old person, we can see that unless the actor has the technique and skill to embody all of the effects of ageing (in the limbs, breath, gaze, degree of muscle tension, and so on) ,the accurate understanding of the physical realities of ageing cannot be perceived by the audience. The yu *enables the* tai *to become visible. They are interdependent. L.M.*

When you rehearse, you must try to be aware of the constant dialogue between these two aspects. There might be a moment when you instinctively grasp something fundamental about a character or situation. You must make sure that this understanding manifests itself as a real influence on what you are doing, moment by moment. This should not be difficult, since as an actor you are always conscious of the surface of your actions, and adapting your expressive actions should be effortless. Equally, if you initiate your explorations by copying external 'phenomena', you must look below the surface in order to discover the deep structure that gives rise to the particular action.

Zeami stresses the importance of an actor understanding the *tai* of a role, and then permitting the *yu* to emerge. This makes sense in traditional Japanese theatre, where the learning method is one of strict imitation of the teacher's external expression, without the student's being told what lies behind these choices. Given this situation, Zeami's advice provides a necessary counterbalance to what could become a very exteriorised style of performance.

In the West, a different situation can emerge. Too often actors focus only on the deep structure of the character or situation, while remaining unaware of what their body is doing at any given moment. In this case, there is a need to work towards a better grasp of the means of expression. Nonetheless, both the Japanese and Western styles of theatre require a constant dialogue between the tai *and the* yu. *L.M.*

RELATIONSHIPS WITH OTHER ACTORS

The next step is to work with other people in order to explore response and relationship. You can take any of the solo exercises such as symmetrical movement, and do them as an exchange with another person. Martial arts movements are also good for this purpose, since all fighting is based on responding to another person. However, there is one difference: the martial arts are based on the need to kill or defend, while the relationship between actors is not based on conflict. Rather the reverse: the contact between actors is an equal and sensitive exchange.

While exploring with other people is a good way to develop real human contact on stage, there is another advantage. If you are improvising on your own, it is hard work to maintain your creativity for more than a few minutes. But with someone else it is far easier. My partner does 'something', and because she has done that action, I am led to do 'something else'. And then, because I have done 'this', my partner can respond with 'that'. Your actions emerge from what your partner has done. Working like this makes it easy to sustain an improvisation.

If you are doing a partnered improvisation (maybe something simple like walking in the same space), and you are not aware of the other person, it looks very odd to the audience. It looks like two completely separate videos being shown at the same moment. There is no relationship between the two people. But when you 'watch' the other person with all of your senses, it becomes a real human exchange.

Being able to respond to other actors and the audience is at the core of Yoshi's work. Not only is the actor expected to be able to 'respond' to inner impulses and link them to the body, he or she must be fully open to what others are doing. Not just to create a pleasant working relationship, but in order to be able to tell the story, moment by moment, as an ensemble.

As a result, when Yoshi teaches, many of his exercises are done in pairs. Not planned or devised pieces, but free improvisations where neither partner 'leads'. Instead, both 'follow', by responding to what has been offered by the other. Usually, this is like a conversation, where each person takes turns in 'speaking'. The 'conversations' may be physical or vocal or both. L M.

Start to walk by getting a sense of your own body, as it is connected to the earth and sky. Then start to move around the room. As you walk about, try to feel the other people in the space. In fact, you are doing two things simultaneously: keeping your awareness of your body in space, and also making contact with other performers. You are using three directions at the same time: up, down, and outwards. Then you imagine that one more 'you' exists in the world, and that this 'you' simply observes what is going on. It observes your physical situation, and it observes how you contact other people. Now you have three levels of activity and awareness: your physical body in space, your relationship with others, and the silent observer.

Two people have a 'conversation', each person using only one hand. As in a real conversation, the partners 'listen' and respond to what the other person is 'saying'. It is not like sign language, or a game of charades, where you try to guess the words. Instead, you try to concentrate your whole existence into that one hand. It is a kind of strange animal, communicating to another equally strange animal. When you find the genuine life of this creature, and it is able to develop a real and varied relationship with the other animal, it is fascinating to watch.

But if we consider what is actually going on here, there is nothing at all. Just two hands twisting, clenching, and wiggling their fingers at each other. What makes it interesting to watch is the relationship between the two tiny 'performers'. The first hand jumps to the side, the other responds with a slow twist, which in turn causes the first hand to quiver for a few seconds. And so on. What is interesting is the exchange. The 'acting' doesn't reside in the hand of each actor; it exists in the air between the two hands. This kind of acting is not narrative, not psychology, not emotion, but something else, something more basic. It is very difficult to describe exactly what it is. But when you watch the exchange between the two hands, something interesting is happening. Something alive.

This is the most fundamental level of acting: the living exchange between two people. When rehearsing, actors very often concentrate on playing the 'situation' of their own individual character, and forget about the other performers. When this happens, it is very hard to discover how to change and develop the scene in any kind of real way. What is missing is the essential exchange between your character and the other characters. In daily life we are constantly exchanging words and actions with other people. This is human reality, and we need to incorporate it into our acting. It is through this living exchange of sound and movement that the story and/or the emotions become visible.

Normally, when you play a particular situation, you try to involve the whole self (body, mind and emotions) in the moment, but it is sometimes interesting to just play around with these three elements. At first, play a given situation with your partner, involving physical responses and words. Then take away the expression in the body and the face, and try to play the scene in exactly the same way. Initially, you will feel that you are simply exchanging psychological responses with your partner, since your body is out of the picture. Nonetheless, your muscles will retain the memory of its physical engagement, and the body will feel alive and alert. This is very important for us to experience as actors. Even when you are not moving, or involving the body in theatrical expression, it mustn't be 'asleep'. In terms of the exercise, you should try to feel that you are 'moving' as strongly as when you were performing the scene with extreme muscular action.

There may be 'nothing' happening with the body, 'nothing' happening with the voice. But there is a great deal of 'movement' on the inside. This is not the same as 'thinking' your way through the scene. In this event, only the thoughts and psychological processes are involved, while the body remains dead. What the above exercise enables us to experience is a kind of invisible physical engagement, where the body 'moves' internally. In this case, the body is fully involved in the scene being played.

Try working on a dialogue scene from a classic text. Normally, actors might try to decide in advance what was 'supposed' to happen in the scene, and then find the appropriate psychological path through the text. Instead, try to forget about the 'meaning' and the emotional situation, and concentrate on two things only. Firstly, to 'sing' the text, making a melody out of the words. And then to enjoy exchanging the melody with the other actor in the scene.

It doesn't matter where the melody goes, sometimes high, sometimes low. Just enjoy the exchange. It isn't a question of creating an interesting sound environment, or making nice music. what matters is that the two actors are really finding the delight in 'human' exchange. And the pleasure of the actors in turn creates pleasure in the audience.

Actors always enjoy themselves on stage. Even when they are murdering each other, or in desolate grief, actors enjoy that situation. This in turn permits the audience to 'enjoy' the performance, despite the possibility that they may be in floods of tears. Actors delight in their relationship with other actors, even when the characters they are playing loathe and detest each other.

And because the actors are really enjoying their exchanges with each other, the audience begins to find the same pleasure in watching and listening to them.

In front of an audience, actors must find ways of making their 'exchange of words' appear believable and natural in terms of the situation of the play. The words have to make sense logically and emotionally. And since it isn't easy to make the words of a text seem completely natural and inevitable, actors spend a lot of time understanding the psychological roots of the character or scene. But if the actors simply look for this aspect of the work and ignore their enjoyment of playing together, there is no deep pleasure for the audience. If we want members of the audience to enjoy themselves on the basic human level as well as the intellectual, actors must find ways of enjoying contact and exchange with their fellow actors. Both levels of performance need to be incorporated: psychological accuracy and the actors' enjoyment. And this must be done through the text or structure of the play.

Naturally, you can't just do anything you feel like on stage. You need to be very clear about exactly what kind of story you are telling the audience, and respect the storyline and world of the play. You mustn't lose sight of your character's essential nature, or forget the reality of his or her situation. Nonetheless, you still can enjoy the freedom of exchange with the other actors. Real life is full of unexpected events, and constantly takes you in unusual directions. Your performance should have the same freshness.

When I talk about 'exchange', I am not exactly certain what is actually exchanged between the actors, or where it comes from. I am sure that it's not the same thing as emotional or psychological understanding. For example, when you 'exchange' sound, it is evident that something more than noise is 'exchanged'. Since the above exercise requires you to respond directly to what your partner offers, without preliminary negotiation (of the style 'If I do this, then you can do that'), you have to work on a level deeper than that of the intellect. As a result, each time you 'exchange', something inside you 'changes' in reaction. From moment to moment, you alter and respond. In this way, as the sounds and movements are exchanged, your inner being constantly shifts.

There is a story about two samurai who lived several centuries ago. They were good friends, but their overlord commanded them to go to different regions. They knew that it would be very difficult to meet again, and were saddened by their parting. In order to preserve their friendship they made a pact. In one year's time they agreed to meet again, at the same place, at exactly the same hour. And so they separated.

They worked hard, and the year passed quickly. One of the samurai returned to the agreed meeting place at the appointed hour. He waited for a while, and then started to worry. What had happened? Had his friend forgotten their promise? But after a few more minutes, there was a knock on the door. He opened it and found his friend standing there.

His friend's face was very pale and he blurted out an apology, explaining that he had been very busy and therefore unable to arrive exactly on time. He continued to apologise, saying that he still had a great deal to do and so could not stay for very long. He seemed uncomfortable, saying that he could not tell his friend why he had to leave so quickly, but insisting that he had to go. He explained that he hadn't wanted to break his promise to his friend, and so had come, if only for a few moments. With one final apology for the brevity of his visit, he departed.

The first samurai was very disappointed and returned home alone. One week later he received a letter from his friend, which read: 'I must apologise to you. I have been working extremely hard and, as a result, had completely lost track of time. I suddenly realised that today was the day that we had agreed to meet, in order to renew our friendship. But the distance between our meeting place and my place of work was a journey of at least three days. I realised that I would be too late. But I had been taught that the spirit could travel faster than the body, so I killed my body. In this way, I hope to arrive at our rendezvous in time to meet you as I had promised.'

The samurai then realised that it was the spirit of his friend that had arrived and then departed so suddenly. And that his friend's spirit had found a way to accomplish what was impossible for the body.

Sometimes, when people do a relationship exercise or improvisation, one of the actors will break off and accuse someone else of blocking the work. They say that if the exercise falls apart, or fails to develop, it is the other person's fault. This kind of thinking isn't helpful. The fault isn't in the other person; if an exercise collapses it is the fault of both actors. But it is always hard to see your own weakness.

It is better to look at things another way. You should completely forget about judging whether someone is better or worse than you. You will get it wrong, and it doesn't help the process. Assume others are the same as you, make contact with them, and then something will happen. You develop together without judgement.

Zeami stresses the importance of considering your own work objectively, and learning from other performers. Even a very good actor will have some weak points, but he or she will be aware of what these are. You should try to be aware of both your strengths and your weaknesses. If you can't perceive your own weaknesses, you will cease to grow as a performer. In addition, you should always watch other actors, even those who are less skilled than yourself, because even an 'inferior' actor will have some good points in their work. Learning from other performers in this way will help you develop new skills and approaches.

One day I said to my Kyogen teacher that I had a friend who wanted to come along and study with him. I explained that I had tried to put this friend off the idea, and my teacher immediately asked why.

'Because he is lazy, and I am sure that he won't persevere,' I replied.

My teacher was furious, and said, 'You are an egotist! Even if your friend only comes once, he could get something of value from the experience. You are trying to do his thinking for him! You are an egotist, and that is why you are not a good actor!'

I hadn't realised that I was an egotist, or that my acting ability was related to this fact. I had thought that if I just kept on training, I would eventually become a good actor. Now I heard that it was my selfish character that was impeding my professional development. So I set about changing my character. I tried to be extremely careful in what I said and did. I attempted to avoid egotistic actions.

But I had also noticed that there were a lot of actors about the place who were extremely egotistical, and yet were very good performers. Equally, there were people who were sweet and generous in nature, but who couldn't act at all. I found this situation most confusing, and started to think about the problem.

People may appear to be egotistical when in fact they are not. A person might simply be concentrating so completely on what he or she is doing, that they are oblivious to the outside world. They don't care about the minor details and rituals of daily existence. To the onlooker, this might seem egocentric. But because these people are fully focused on their own performance, they appear to be good actors.

On the other hand, people who seem kind and considerate might be totally in love with themselves. They desperately want to be appreciated, and therefore worry about other people's opinions and criticisms. They don't want to be seen to be a difficult person, and are constantly thinking about how they are viewed. And because they are always focused on their effect on other people, they can't give their full attention to what is really happening around them. In terms of acting, this type of individual can't concentrate on what should happen during the performance. Instead, they constantly worry about externals. And this affects the quality of their acting.

Nonetheless, I suspect that the first kind of actor (the 'egotistical' type) cannot become a truly great performer. At a certain point it becomes evident that something needs to change.

Somehow, in order to be a great actor, you have to develop a balance between yourself and the outside world. You need to concentrate fully on yourself and what you are doing, but at the same time, you mustn't be oblivious to the world around you. You have to develop an awareness that extends beyond yourself. But this awareness of other people is not the same as dependence on their good opinion. You are untroubled by criticism, and don't try to do things in order to make people like you.

Instead, you try to find a harmony between your own inner focus and the awareness of the outside world. You do what you need to do for yourself, while at the same time you unify yourself with other people. This is an easy, unconscious process; you don't need to think about it. You concentrate fully on your task, while unconsciously responding to the people around you. There is a balance between yourself and others.

In the martial arts, the prime aim is self-protection. If you are in a fight, the only way you can save yourself is by defeating your opponent. And in some cases, the only way to defeat him is by killing him. If, during a duel, you are thinking about your survival, you are unlikely to win, since you are concentrating on something other than the ebb and flow of the combat. Instead, you should just focus on the relationship with your opponent, and the simple actions and responses, such as: 'He is coming from above, I must turn this way. He is attacking from there, where is the opening?'

If, in addition, you are thinking, 'I want to survive!' you won't be able to find this kind of concentration. You won't be able to manipulate the exchange of combat. The secret is simple: you can only win when you are ready to die.

It is the same in theatre. Many of us become actors because we want to be successful, or we need the audience's applause. But if you want to receive applause, you have to give up the idea of getting it. This is incredibly difficult, since wanting applause is part of being an actor.

OUR RELATIONSHIP WITH THE AUDIENCE

There is another important human exchange: between the actor and the audience. This is very clear when you are doing a solo performance. In the absence of other performers, the 'exchange' occurs directly between the performer and the audience. Like a storyteller, the solo actor *enjoys* the relationship with the onlookers and responds to changes in their emotions. For example, if the audience starts to feel sad, the actor can choose to lead them into further sadness, or to reverse the mood.

Zeami also offered actors some advice on how to respond to the audience. He recommended that each day, before entering on to the stage, the actors should try to 'feel' the audience, since every day is different. This is less easy to judge today, with the modern design of theatres and the large size of contemporary audiences, but nonetheless you should still attempt to get a sense of who you will be playing to. Some days you think, 'This is going to be uphill work,' while other days you know that the audience will enable you to perform well. This ability to sense the audience is something that you acquire with experience.

Once you have gained a sense of how the audience is feeling, you must then adjust your acting accordingly. If, for example, you have a huge crowd and they are excited and noisy, the theatre's atmosphere is not calm. In this case you should wait a little, until they start to wonder when the show is going to start. Minute by minute their attention becomes more focused on the stage (instead of their private conversations) and they become increasingly eager for the performance to begin. At that exact moment, you start the show.

Obviously there are occasions when you cannot delay the start even if the audience are over-exuberant. The moment arrives and you have to start. In this case you must perform very strongly: speak the text powerfully, and make the movements and action very clear and defined. This will make the audience calm down and focus their attention on the performance.

According to Zeami, these styles of audience response are linked to the ideas of Yin and Yang. Even the time of day when you perform has an effect on your style. Since daytime is Yang, your performing style should be Yin, in order to maintain the appropriate balance. In contrast, the night is Yin, and so requires a more Yang style of acting. For Yang acting, you should play more strongly, making clear decisions which are communicated with energy and power. Yin acting is more interior and less extravagant in expression.

The tempo of performance also changes. At night, you should perform slightly faster, while during the day you can afford to slow down. These theories of Yin and Yang are very useful to performers, even though you should be careful not to apply them too rigidly. If you say that nighttime is always Yin, you may miss the fact that on one particular evening the audience is extremely lively (i.e. Yang), and your performance would be completely inappropriate. The important thing is to be aware of exactly how the audience is reacting on that particular occasion, and then to construct your performance accordingly, in order to maintain the correct balance.

When I was performing the *Mahabharata*, I had to pay great attention to the state of the audience, since one of my major scenes would have been ruined if I had been careless. In this scene, my character, Drona, committed suicide in a very calm and deliberate way. The scene before was broad comedy. If the audience was still laughing (i.e. geared up for comedy) when I entered, I would play the beginning of the scene very slowly in order to calm them down, and to change the focus of their emotions. The amount of laughter varied from night to night, and the way I initiated the scene altered in response. I did not change what I was doing, merely adjusted the tempo and force of my acting in order to bring the audience into a suitably receptive state. In this way they would be able to respond to the theme and atmosphere of that particular scene.

In my experience, it is very important not to spend the time before the start of the show sitting in the dressing room. You must go out and 'smell' what kind of audience you have that night. Then you can react appropriately. Even before making your entrance on to the stage, you should try to sense what has happened between the start of the play and your appearance. I always try to watch the play from the wings or the back of the audience in order to be in touch with what is happening.

Brook says that performing a play is like storytelling, with several people sharing the responsibility. I understand this idea, since the tradition of storytelling is very strong in Japan (and is one of the areas in which I trained). In Japan, there is normally only one storyteller, who has to stay constantly aware of the audience and to adjust his performance accordingly in order to keep the story alive and enthralling. He controls the audience. When the audience becomes Yin, he employs more of a Yang style, and vice versa. A Western-style play requires the same skills, but the responsibility for telling the story is spread among a number of performers.

Too often actors sit in their dressing rooms or in the green room, listening to the tannoy for their cues. Once they hear the stage manager call their name, they go up (or down) into the wings, ready to make their entrance. Not only does this practice make it difficult to sense the audience, it is also completely unhelpful in terms of good storytelling. There is only *one* story being told by a team of actors; not ten different stories being told by ten actors. Therefore, you need to be there in the wings from the very beginning, in order to see how the other actors are telling the story. In this way, you can see what you will have to do in order to pick up the story and carry it forward when it is your turn to act. You might have to carefully pick up a subtle mood and continue it without changing the flow. Equally, you might have to sharply break a mood in order to refocus the audience's attention. There are no clear rules about this, except that you have to ensure that the story is told accurately and well, and, as an actor, you must be able to adjust your performance in order to ensure that this happens. Only by watching and listening can you work out what you need to do each night.

In the Noh theatre, they have a saying: 'You must unify one thousand eyes.' This means that the fundamental points of your performance should have the same impact on all the onlookers. Everyone should basically agree about what they are seeing.

4 Speaking

BREATHING

In ordinary daily life, breathing is an unconscious activity, you just do it without thinking. Some parts of the body are moved by our conscious will, whereas other parts work without our mental control. Normally, breathing is one of these involuntary actions, yet at the same time we know that we can control the mechanism of breath when we want to. It is the only mechanism that works in both ways. Through the use of conscious breathing exercises we can link into unconscious activity, which in turn connects us to the unconscious world of the mind. Maybe this is why deciding to breathe deeply and fully makes you feel good: somehow more alive. In everyday life we very rarely use the full range of the lungs, so you should try to explore all of your lung capacity when you do breathing exercises.

When we are asleep we breathe in and out continuously. When we die, the breath stops. These three basic breathing patterns (in, out, and stopped), are what exist in ordinary life, and since theatre aims to evoke the genuine experience of real life, these are the patterns we employ on the stage. We must think about when we breathe in and when we breathe out, and where we stop the breath.

This is not simply to help us say long speeches without running out of air; changes of breath have an inner impact. To see how this works, try breathing in, then stop the breath for a couple of seconds, then breathe out. Now do it the other way round: breathe out, stop the breath, and then breathe in. You will probably notice that the physical or emotional sensation is slightly different.

When you walk, try to maintain a neutral body, and think about linking it to your breathing; for example, breathe in prior to walking, breathe out while walking. Or breathe out before starting, breathe in while walking, stop and hold the breath while you are still, and then let it out when you start moving again. Experiment with the various possibilities. You will discover that each pattern corresponds to a different feeling or mood.

One of the secret techniques of the Noh theatre involves knowing when to stop the breath. For example, when you rise from sitting to standing, you inhale while in the sitting position, then block the breath, and rise without breathing out. Sometimes, in the past, older Noh actors died onstage as a result of using this technique, so you have to be careful when employing it. But it does illustrate the point that acting does not just involve breathing in and out; it also involves the use of the held breath. The trick is knowing the exact moment to hold the breath in terms of dramatic action.

Take a small section of text, maybe only one or two lines, and experiment with some of the following breath patterns. Breathe in, and then say the words slowly as you exhale. Next, try a slow breath out, quickly inhale, and then speak. As you alter the relationship between the speech and the breathing, you will find that different feelings emerge quite naturally. Breath is very closely connected to emotion, and changing the breath pattern will alter the emotional response.

In terms of performance, you can use this insight to help you create truthful reactions. For example, if you have to portray the act of stabbing someone, then the accurate pattern for this action is 'breathe in, then strike the blow'. Reproduce that breathing pattern, and the audience is more likely to find the action believable (and a truthful emotion may appear of its own accord). Of course, if you are using this technique, you must discover the exact and correct breathing pattern for each activity. Otherwise it doesn't work.

To help us develop our breathing, there are a number of exercises we can use. These are derived from traditional practice, and often employ the use of images. One of them involves thinking about our skin.

Stand or sit comfortably with your back straight, breathe in slowly through the nose, breathe out through the mouth, but as you breathe out imagine that the air passes out through the pores of the skin. Continue this exercise for several minutes. To develop this further, imagine that the air enters the body through the navel and exits through the pores.

You can now add another image to the exercise: as the air leaves the body, it streams out from the pores in the form of white vapour. Obviously, you are always actually breathing through the nose and mouth, but by visualising the breath in different parts of the body, it seems to open up other possibilities.

There is an old saying: 'Ordinary people breathe through the chest, wise people breathe through the hara, and the skilled person breathes through the feet.'

The 'wise person' refers to the practice of meditation; if you do this, concentrate your breathing in the hara, the area just below your navel. The 'skilled person' is someone who uses their body in a highly developed way, such as an actor, or martial artist. People in these fields use the image of getting energy from the earth to help them.

Imagine that air is entering your body through the feet, then it travels to the hara. Exhale, and visualise the breath leaving the body through the *tan-den* (the core point of the hara, about three centimetres below the navel), and travelling far into the distance. Again, you are working on two levels: the physical intake and expulsion of air through the lungs, and the image used to focus the breathing.

Another exercise uses imaginary sounds. When you breathe in, *imagine* that you are saying 'aaaah', and that when you breathe out you use the sound 'aawm' (or 'ohm'). You can reverse the sounds, 'aaaah' on the out-breath, and 'aawm' as you inhale.

You can combine these exercises: for example, breathing in through the navel, while making the imaginary sound 'aaaa', and out through the pores, with the imaginary sound 'aawm'.

You can then start to experiment with a real 'voiced' sound on the out-breath, using these various combinations. For example, breathe in with imaginary 'aawm' through the navel, and out with the real sound 'aaah' through the navel. *(In this exercise, the mouth obviously produces the real sound 'aawm', but in your imagination it emerges through the navel. L.M.)* There are many possibilities: take the time to explore each one fully, and note the subtle differences between them.

As well as the navel and the *tan-den*, there are other points on the body that you can use to focus the breathing. These include a point on the sternum. You find this point on your chest by placing your little finger in your navel and then stretching your hand up until your thumb rests on the sternum. The place where your thumb is resting is the point you use to focus your breathing.

Another exercise concentrates on the nostrils. Breathe in through the left nostril, and out through the right. Then reverse the process: in through the right and out through the left. This can be done through visualisation, or by pressing your finger against the opposite nostril in order to hold it shut.

The following series of breathing exercises uses more abstract images to emphasise the inner connection.

Breathe in, and when you have fully expanded the lungs, stop the breath and tighten the anus. At that moment, imagine that the air you have taken in is mixing itself with the stale air already in your body. Then breathe out, and visualise the mixed air leaving. Continue this exercise until you feel that all the old stale air has been replaced with fresh air. In addition, when you 'take' the air into your body, don't imagine you are 'sucking' or 'grabbing'. Rather, imagine that there is a vast, generous world of energy out there which freely gives you air. You 'receive' the air, you don't 'take' it. This may seem a small quibble over vocabulary, but there is a huge difference in terms of effect.

The next set of three exercises come from T'ai Chi. Standing with your feet shoulder-width apart, your legs slightly bent, and your back straight, breathe slowly in and out. As you breathe in, imagine that air rises up from the earth via the legs. As you breathe out, imagine that the air returns to the earth (also through the legs). A similar exercise demands that you visualise the air travelling up your spine on the in-breath. As you breathe in, the air rises up the spine, continues across the top of the skull, and then arrives at the point between your eyebrows. You then breathe out while imagining that the air is descending past your mouth, your sternum, your navel, and then it simply dissipates. As you breathe in again, the cycle recommences. In the next exercise, the same cycle begins and ends at the feet: the air enters from the earth, travels up the back of the body, goes across the crown of the head, down to the *tan-den*, and then disappears.

You can also use sound to stimulate your breathing. Choose a repetitive sound, like a metronome or the waves of the sea, or alternatively a pure sound like a note held note on a flute. You then imagine that this sound enters your body via the pores as you breathe in, and then air exits through the mouth or *tan-den* as you breathe out. Or you can switch it round so that air enters on the in-breath, and the sound exits on the out-breath. You can do it any way round you like. Each way is different, but all are equally useful. Just experiment, and see what happens.

These are fairly complicated breathing exercises; an easier one is to breathe normally, and simply observe yourself breathing. I also recommend that you watch how a baby breathes. Babies take slow, deep breaths and their whole abdomen seems to expand gently as they breathe in. They provide a very good example for us to follow.

And now for an even more complicated breathing exercise. This one involves placing the hands in specific positions as the exercise progresses. Stand, or sit, and extend your arms horizontally in front of you, so that the palms of your hands face each other, and are about two centimetres apart. The thumbs face towards the ceiling. As you breathe in, the air enters through the fingertips and travels up the arms into the body. As you breathe out, the process is reversed. You also fix your gaze on a point between the two palms, and as you continue to breathe in and out, you may find that the hands eventually drift together. When and if this happens, close your eyes and continue breathing in the same way. To finish the exercise, take a deep in-breath, hold it for a couple of seconds, relax, and let the hands fall, palm upwards, to the sides of your body. You then open your eyes, and breathe out to finish.

In all these exercises, it is important to stay tall and relaxed, even when you are sitting. The spine and neck are gently stretching up, and you should try to maintain your body in a vertical position relative to the floor. It is easier if you close your eyes, since you are less likely to be distracted by outside events. In this way you can just keep concentrating on your imagination and your breathing. Or if you prefer to keep your eyes open, you can lower your gaze, so that you are focusing on a point at forty-five degrees down to the floor. This also helps cut out distractions. These exercises can be done in a number of positions: standing, sitting in a chair, or sitting on the floor, but, whichever way you choose, you must pay attention to the position of your upper body. I have already mentioned that it needs to be fully vertical (don't let it slump), but it also needs to be symmetrical (don't let it twist or lean to one side). Some traditions maintain that through this kind of breathing exercise we place our bodies into contact with exterior sources of energy, and for this we must have a proper body position. In any event, the vertical yet relaxed body is a useful basic form for everyone, but it is especially valuable for actors.

A final note on using breath. In general exercises, we breathe in through the nose and out through the mouth. But in both Yoga training and certain African dance traditions, the mouth should be kept closed at all times, so that the air always travels via the nose. In Benin, even when the dancer is performing with enormous force and speed, the mouth is held firmly shut. It is a different use of breath, and gives a particular quality to the performance.

Another advantage of breathing exercises is that they enable you to calm down, even when you are feeling fear.

You always have fear when you are on stage. My own long history of fear began quite early. When I began to perform, around the age of fifteen, I never felt even the tiniest bit nervous. But as soon as I decided to make a serious career out of acting, the fear arrived. The first attack came after a performance was over. While I was actually on stage, I had no memory of what was happening, but afterwards, between finishing and going to sleep, I found myself trembling.

Extreme fear is a problem, since it renders you completely helpless. You can barely move, far less perform well. If you suffer this severely, and can't work through your fear, it is probably better to give up theatre, and find a less 'dangerous' profession. But I suspect that, in reality, fear is very close to excitement. Some people say that if you have no fear, you perform better. I don't agree. I have seen a lot of actors who are never nervous, but they can be incredibly boring to watch: the performance becomes mechanical, and there is no energy on the stage. Other actors, who are so overwhelmed with fear that they can hardly manage to step on to the stage, are totally fascinating. They grab your full attention. Fear is not necessarily a negative element. You have to go with fear (and its associated stomach pain).

It is interesting to consider why we experience fear. When I was a young actor, I thought that I was always making mistakes, and this made me rather nervous. Other people have a strong desire to 'be successful'. But 'being successful' depends on other people's perceptions of your work, and so you start to worry about what 'they' are thinking. We all know that we really shouldn't care about what people think, but unfortunately we do care. And this makes us afraid.

So what can we do prevent debilitating fear? Before a show, have a drink of water, go to the toilet, do some breathing exercises, then stand in front of a mirror and say to yourself: 'I am a good actor. I am a very good actor. I am a Great Actor!'

Fear can give you an extraordinary energy. Don't refuse it: learn to employ it. Try to turn it into its positive form: theatrical excitement.

The house next door is on fire. You rush into the blazing building to save the furniture (you have already rescued the children and the cat). You carry out the armchair and the valuable sideboard. Two hours later, once the fire has been extinguished, you decide to shift the furniture to a more convenient spot. But you can't lift the chair; suddenly it is far too heavy. Under the stress and panic of a serious situation, an amazing power appears in your body. Panic, like imagination, can change your body.

When I was in Africa, I had an experience like this. Peter Brook had taken a group of actors on a journey across the Sahara in order to study how theatre operated outside modern Westernised society. As part of this research, we would perform improvised scenes in remote villages, to people with whom we had no common language. One day, I was completely carried away in the improvisation, and suddenly performed a flying somersault. But I don't know how to do a somersault! It's not one of my skills. Yet somehow I did it. I remember thinking, as I jumped around in front of the villagers, 'I've got to do *something*!' And unconsciously my body found a way to do an action that is normally beyond me.

SOUND

Now we start to explore our voice.

Choose a position that is comfortable. Sitting or standing, it doesn't matter, as long as you are not lying down. You should always have the feeling that your spine is in a line of connection between the sky and the centre of the earth. Then close your eyes, and try to imagine that you are newly born, just emerged from your mother's womb. You are innocent and without conscious intelligence. Like water. And when babies sleep, they have a very slow, deep breathing pattern. You observe that same breathing pattern in your own body. Don't imitate a child, or try to act as if you are a baby: you are yourself, but with the breath of a baby. After a while, you develop the breath into a gentle sound. Each time you breathe out, you permit the sound 'ssss' to emerge. Then, after a minute or so, the sound 'ssss' transforms into the sound 'mmmm'. This is still a relaxed, innocent sound.

After spending a bit of time just making the sound 'mmmm', gently let the head drop backwards, until your face looks to the sky. As the head sinks backwards, the mouth will naturally fall open, and the sound will transform into 'aaah'. When you breathe in, return the head to the basic position (with the face looking straight ahead).

Now, we engage the imagination. You try to feel as if the sound 'aaah' does not originate in your body. Instead you imagine that the sound 'aaah' already exists far away, up in the sky. It is a huge sound that has existed for centuries. You then imagine that your own personal 'aaah' sound travels into the sky, and unifies with the already existing 'aaah'. You don't try to 'project' your 'aaah' with muscular effort; it is your imagination that does the work. Physical force has limitations, so it is better to use your will and imagination, which have no limitations.

We will now go in the opposite direction. Make your 'mmmm' sound in the basic position (face looking forwards), then let the head drop forwards towards the earth. Your mouth will need to widen as the jaw compresses, and the sound will transform into 'eeee'. When you make the 'eeee' sound, imagine that you are unifying your personal 'eeee' with an enormous 'eeee' that exists at the centre of the earth.

In a sense, 'eeee' is an artificial sound: it doesn't happen without a certain conscious effort, unlike 'aaah'. 'Aaah' is very natural: babies all over the world produce this sound instinctively. It is also interesting to note that many cultures attach similar meanings to the baby's 'ma ma' sound. In Europe, it is linked to the concept of 'mother', while in Japan, 'ma ma' means 'food'. Babies always start with the 'aaah' sound, not 'eeee'. It is far easier for the body to produce.

Now we have two sounds: 'aaah' towards the sky, and 'eeee' towards the earth. But why isn't it the opposite way round? To find the answer, you can try an experiment. Stand naturally. Get someone (or two someones) to grip your body, and ask them to lift you straight up, so that your feet come off the ground. The first time, just do it normally, so that you get a sense of how much you actually weigh. The second time, when you are lifted, make the sound 'aaah' (you don't need to drop the head back; just making the sound is enough). When you make the sound 'aaah', imagine that you are unifying yourself with the huge 'aaah' in the sky.

Return your feet to the ground, and then repeat the lift again, this time making the sound 'eeee'. When you make the 'eeee', connect with the 'eeee' deep inside the earth.

You (and your lifters) will probably find that you appear 'heavier' with the 'eeee' sound, to the point that you are quite difficult to get off the ground. Conversely, your body is lighter than normal with the 'aaah' sound. There is no real logic to this phenomenon, but something appears to change according to the sound you produce, and this change is linked to particular directions in space.

In daily life, you can use these sounds to help you shift loads. When lifting something from the ground, make the sound 'eeeyaah'. The sound moves from earth to sky, and this is in sympathy with the action you are undertaking. If you use the sound to help you, the task becomes easier. When pulling something downwards, the sound 'aahyeee' is useful. If you attempt to do it the other way round, you will notice the difference. Saying 'aahyeee' when trying to lift something feels unnatural, and it is harder to accomplish the task. Somehow, the sound changes you and your body.

Looking at the overall pattern of sound and direction, we have 'aaah' linked to straight up, and 'eeee' to straight down. And the initial sound 'mmmm' (or a soft 'oooo' sound made with relaxed lips) is situated inside yourself; it is interior and personal, like a baby sleeping. But there are two more sounds to consider: 'aaw' (pronounced like the 'o' in the English word 'or') and 'eh' (pronounced like the 'e' in the English word 'set'). The direction for 'aaw' lies forty-five degrees below the direction for 'aaah'. In this way, the sound 'aaw' cuts into the air, midway between the horizon and the sky. The next sound 'eh' is placed about ten degrees below the horizontal. Now we have four directions: descending from the sky to the earth, they are: 'aaah', 'aaw', 'eh' and 'eeee'.

When you look at words used in religious ritual, they often seem to incorporate these key sounds and directions. In Japanese, the word used for 'God' is *Kami*, which is pronounced 'kah-mee'. The sound therefore 'travels' from the sky, into the interior of the speaker, and then descends into the earth ('K-aah-mm-ee'). The Hebrew word 'Jehovah', which is pronounced 'yeh-haw-vah', starts just below the horizon, and then rises through the diagonal into the sky. The Latin Amen, 'Aah-mm-ehn', comes from the sky, enters the speaker, and then goes out into the world again. One of the names of the planet, 'Gaia', shows a similar pattern. Pronounced 'Gah-ee-yaah', the sound travels from the sky to the earth, and then back out to the sky again.

Even in daily life, we use this principle. Most cultures have work-songs or chants that help people to dig, or to row, or to haul in nets.

These function as a means of coordinating rhythmic effort within a group, but the sounds chosen for this purpose tend to incorporate the 'directions' mentioned above. In English, 'heave' is the best known example. This sound/word, lengthened to 'heeeeve', is used for actions requiring a lot of physical effort. In this case, focusing on the strength of the earth through the 'eee' sound seems to make the job easier. Since these sounds get chosen as an aid to physical activity, there seems to be some kind of energy involved in the connection.

In Japanese classical theatre, the voice is created and used in a different way than in the West. When speaking text, both Noh and Kabuki use heightened speech patterns, and archaic language. In the Noh theatre, the language is so old-fashioned that very few ordinary Japanese people can understand the words or their meaning. In addition, sounds are elongated or given unusual intonations. What Westerners would describe as naturalistic speech is not used in the traditional theatres.

Some sections of a play might be 'sung', although this resembles chanted song, rather than the Western operatic approach. Both Noh and Kabuki provide musical accompaniment to the performance, and the tonal range of these instruments is the same as the human voice. In this way, they enhance and reinforce the vocal expressivity of the actor, creating a kind of sound 'landscape'; not quite music, but not normal speech either.

The Japanese concept of a 'beautiful voice' is also slightly different to Western ideals. It is not liquid purity, nor melodious tones, that are highly valued; rather the ability to suggest and heighten a range of emotions, moods and atmospheres.

Within the esoteric religions of Japan, sounds and chants play an important role in the process of spiritual development. Part of this is the 'repetition' that Yoshi has already discussed, but there is another reason. According to certain religious traditions (such as Shingon Buddhism) some sounds have special qualities, and through repeating these sounds inner transformation is promoted. Sometimes, it is a single sound, sometimes a word, or a Mantra.

When doing vocal work derived from whichever Japanese tradition, remember that the vowels are all 'pure' (i.e. not diphthongs). There are five of these vowel sounds: 'A' (pronounced 'ah' as in the English word 'far'), 'O' (pronounced 'aw' as in the English word 'or', 'U' (pronounced 'oo', but with relaxed lips: the Japanese do not have strong sound 'oo', as in 'soon', made with pursed lips), 'E' (pronounced like the 'e' in set'), and 'I' (pronounced 'ee' as in 'see'). L.M.

You can also improvise with this work. Try to imagine a body position 'aah'. You can create this shape using your whole body, or only one part, such as the hand. Or even just one finger. Then make the shape that corresponds to 'eee', and then 'aaw'. You will find that the quality of each sound demands a specific shape, and these shapes are different from each other. The shapes that the sounds produce will vary from person to person. There is no standard form, and everyone's response to the sounds will be personal and unique. And each sound/shape will 'feel' different inside.

When I say 'feel', I am referring to 'body sensation', not simply emotion. Everything you do and say has its own distinct 'flavour', and this 'flavour' is not the same as emotion or psychology. It is the inner echo of what the body is doing. And every time the body changes what it is doing, the inner 'flavour' shifts as well.

While this phenomenon is interesting to study, it is more important to find its practical use to you as an actor. For example, since the sounds 'aaah' and 'eee' have different qualities, they will give you different physical sensations. When you make the sounds, taste them, and observe how the inner dimension changes. Notice each sound's particular character. Then you can add other sounds such as 't', 's', 'k', to create the sounds 'kah', 'kee', 'mah', and so on. Depending on which consonant you choose, the feeling of 'aah' will change: 'tah', 'kah', 'mah', 'sah'.

Once again, we can see that many languages incorporate these sound elements into their word choices, especially the verbs. Here is an exercise. Say the following two words several times, really 'tasting' their physical sensation: 'aaaw-soo' and 'hee-koo'. Keep saying them for a while. In fact, these are Japanese verbs. One means 'push' and the other means 'pull'. Try to guess which is which. Most people feel that 'aaaw-soo' (transcribed as *osu*) is 'push' and 'hee-koo' (transcribed as *hiku*) is 'pull'. This is correct. There is a connection between the 'taste' of the sound and its sense of meaning.

Be careful of one thing when you do this exercise. You must taste the quality of sound through the muscles of the body and through its echo in the emotions. It is not an 'idea' of what the sound might mean. (*If you find yourself saying something like, 'It is the sort of sound that a person might make if they were pushing', you are on the wrong track. This is an intellectual 'idea' about the sound, rather than a direct physical response to its particular energy. Keep it simple. L.M.*)

According to Japanese esoteric Buddhism, when you are born, you make the simple clear sound 'aaaah' like a god. As time passes, and you become 'educated' and skilled in responding to the demands of society, you become a character with an appropriate vocal style. The open clear 'aaah' is gone. And then you spend the rest of your life, working to recover the first pure 'aaah', hoping to retrieve your innate divinity.

TEXT

A philosopher of language once said that in the beginning, everybody on earth spoke the same language. Afterwards, as each culture developed, the languages separated. Somehow, I feel that this is true, because the basic sound-sense of a language can often be grasped, even where you can't understand the literal meaning of the words.

Sounds have their own resonances or 'meanings'. A good writer, either consciously or unconsciously, writes more than a story, more than speeches or dialogue. A good writer chooses sounds. When you pronounce the words of a great writer (like Shakespeare), even without understanding the language, you feel something, because he has chosen the right sounds. When acting, we need to incorporate this respect for sound as a part of our work on text. Next time you are given some lines, try this experiment. Before exploring the meaning of each phrase, or the emotional content, or the social situation, try to simply 'taste' the sounds. If the author has chosen these sounds, we must respect them. But if you are too preoccupied with emotion, you may forget to think about this dimension.

Let me give a simple example of the potency of sounds. Remember the earlier exercise where you made the sound 'ha ha ha'? If you keep going long enough, you start to feel happy. In fact, in Kyogen, this is how you are taught to communicate laughter in a performance. You just make the sound 'ha ha ha', and you start to feel cheerful. The sounds 'shaay, shaay, shaay' are used in the same way for sadness.

I have also noticed that the sound 'eeee', provokes a tight, closed, 'painful' inner feeling. (*Perhaps this is why the English language uses this sound in the word 'keening', to describe the vocal expression of mourning, and in the word 'grief'. L.M.*)

These examples are fairly simple, and not all words follow this pattern. Many of the words we use in daily life are 'technical', and have no emotional correspondence. They simply describe things, or provide information. Equally, a lot of words have changed their meanings over time, and any connection between the sound and its inner echo has been lost. Nonetheless, there are still hundreds of words that carry an emotional resonance in their sound, and, as I said above, a good writer will incorporate this dimension in the text. For this reason, you should always try to 'taste' the sounds of the writer's words, since these may help you to connect to the emotional quality of the script.

When the company was rehearsing the *Mahabharata* with Peter Brook, we spent a lot of time working on English pronunciation with an English actor. He chose some lines from Shakespeare as the basis for the exercises. I couldn't understand the meaning of these words, but through speaking the sounds, I began to get a feel for the world of the play, and of Shakespeare's characters.

Even with a bad writer, you should still work this way. You must respect the sound of the text, and not make decisions about how to play it in advance. A lot of people say to themselves, 'This is what I feel about Shakespeare, so this is how I will speak the lines.' Or, 'This is a bad writer, so I will do it this way, in order to make it more interesting.' If you think like this, you are not respecting the text. You must follow the intentions of the author, and you must also respect the sounds of the words that he or she has chosen. Then you can discover something beyond the simple storyline.

Since the sounds of words have strong emotional qualities, playing the same part in different languages feels different. Some of Peter Brook's productions, such as the *Mahabharata* and *The Man Who*, were performed in both French and English, and I played the same role in both. The words of the text had the same meaning, but very different sound qualities, and so inevitably my performance altered. The quality of the sound limits you, and shapes your interpretation. For example, in *Hamlet* the word 'vengeance' is often used. In Japanese, the same word is *hukushu*, but the sound is very different. You cannot play *hukushu* with the same edge as 'vengeance'. Different sounds evoke different inner responses, and your performance alters accordingly.

Therefore, the quality of the translation affects the whole production. Not only does a bad translation confuse or corrupt the storyline, and produce phrases that are difficult for the actors to speak, but also the words chosen for the translation will affect the actor's inner landscape.

There is another element: the sounds of the words will alter the audience's perception of the character.

In a certain sense, there is no such thing as 'a character'; there is only the accumulation of details, which the audience then interprets as the traits of a specific personality. These 'details' include how the person stands and moves, what words they choose to communicate with, how rapidly they respond to the situations presented, and so on. Using these elements, the audience gradually paints a picture, which finally reveals itself to be 'that person'. When the details change, the audience's interpretation automatically shifts. If the translation is bad, and does not take the importance of sound into account, the words will have a completely different resonance, and the audience will have the impression of another personality.

Even in the case of an identical story (and production) in English and French, there is a completely different feeling to the performance. Even the accent creates a different impression. When you look at the performances of an actor who speaks both French and English equally well, you get the impression that the entire personality has shifted between the two versions. Obviously, the personality hasn't really changed, but it looks as if it has because the 'details' have altered. L.M.

When you experiment with sounds and feelings as part of working on a text, you must not lose sight of the logical structure of each sentence. The words must always make sense, no matter what you do with your voice or emotions. I play with a huge number of vocal possibilities, but at the same time I carefully follow the grammar, in order to ensure that I am communicating something very specific. In this way, the words become my own, not merely clichéd responses.

Because I am dreadful at speaking English and French, I can't play big parts in Peter Brook's productions. Being such a poor linguist annoys me from time to time, but I do have certain advantages as a foreigner when I approach text. When I speak lines in a foreign language, I have to pay great attention to the logic of the phrase, otherwise I can't understand it. I have to look for the grammar, and I need to see how the sentence is constructed. But when I speak Japanese, I don't think about grammar or the logic of the phrase, I simply speak the lines. And they usually emerge as a kind of 'melody' that incorporates all the worst clichés and mannerisms of bad theatre. It becomes a kind of 'imitation', rather than something that is my own genuine human response. I am simply imitating somebody else's melody that I have heard in daily life, or reproducing theatre tradition. If you only have a melody without following the underlying logic of the lines, you may be able to seduce the audience but you won't be able to create the sense of a real human being.

A couple of years ago I went back to Japan to do a film in which I played the role of an old samurai warrior. As soon as I received the script, I could hear all the old clichéd ways of speaking that you find in most samurai films. This conventional way of speaking is very hard to avoid. Yet no one knows how these warriors spoke three hundred years ago. All we have are the stereotypes we see on film and television, which have no direct connection to the truth of the situation. I had to work really hard in order to avoid clichés and to make these lines come alive for me.

If you are working on a specific piece of text, try playing around with changes in breathing, or pitch, or volume, when saying the lines. You will find that, according to what you do with your voice (speaking softly, or slowly, or with variations in breathing), different situations and responses will emerge. You can play with feeling in the same way. For example, you say your lines as if the events you are describing make you feel sad. Then you repeat the same lines as if they provoke anger. Or you can say them as if you find the whole thing hilariously funny. This is not a question of 'colouring' the text with a wash of emotion, but rather finding a different emotional reaction to the events that the text is describing. Normally, actors explore only one emotional possibility when learning their lines; the one that is suggested by an understanding of the psychology of the scene. But rather than pre-selecting your emotional response in this way, try experimenting with arbitrary choices, and then see what each one offers.

In Japan, it is said that a good storyteller won't have a particularly beautiful voice. If you have a beautiful voice, you feel safe, and as a consequence, you don't work hard enough at getting the story across.

There is a story about a Bunraku narrator, who lived in Japan about a hundred years ago. At this time, some of the ideas of Western naturalistic theatre were filtering into Japanese performances. According to traditional storytelling practice, narrators simply attempted to say their lines in a loud, beautiful voice. But this man had a rather poor voice, and these Western concepts helped him to find a way of solving the problem. Instead of speaking with elegance and sonority, he tried to reproduce each character, giving a sense of their personal psychology in a more realistic way. He rapidly became a star, since the Japanese intelligentsia of that period identified with this new approach.

REFLECTING REALITY

Contrast and variety are necessary for the audience, since it is not possible for them to remain engaged with the performance if it remains locked on any one level. However, the need for contrast lies deeper than merely keeping the audience entertained. It is essential for creating theatre that is true to human life.

In our daily existence there are many changes of rhythm, pace and direction. We may sit still for several minutes, then suddenly jump to our feet, and then wander into the kitchen to make a cup of tea. Even in a short period of time there will be a range of different actions and responses. Theatre needs to reflect this constantly shifting variety in order to appear truthful. In addition, all theatre compresses time. Events taking place over ten years, ten months, or a couple of days are squeezed into a show lasting a few hours at most. On stage, it is the *essence* of events that is reproduced, not every single detail. Even a supposedly 'naturalistic' playwright like Chekhov does not write in 'real time', he merely creates this illusion. Subconsciously the audience 'knows' that they are seeing a distillation of events rather than an exact reproduction. Since the passage of even a single day holds a huge variety of actions, a production needs to maintain a similar range of contrasting rhythms. This creates a performance that is experienced as a believable reflection of 'real life'.

Even if in daily life we move slowly, then pause for a long time, and move slowly again, this does not appear 'truthful' on stage, because it contradicts the shifts and changes that the audience recognises as 'real life'. This is why actors need to understand the importance of rhythm and tempo when constructing their performance. An accurate reproduction of an emotional moment might feel very truthful to the actor, but it won't necessarily look truthful to the viewer. Before you think about generating an emotion, you should examine what you need to do in terms of rhythm and timing. In fact, if you construct your tempo properly, the emotion will arise quite easily.

It is important that theatre works with compressed time. Otherwise, you simply have a section of life cut out and placed on view. People see daily life all the time, they don't need to come to the theatre for this. They come to the theatre for something more.

As an actor, I need to be free of the text. I don't want to worry about which line comes next when I am performing. If it is a long text, it is necessary to understand its basic structure. Where does it begin? Which is the main section? Where is the end? You can't just go on and on and on through the text as if it were all the same. Like a mystery novel, it has structure. And like a mystery novel, it is sometimes helpful to look at the ending in order to work out the beginning. If the ending is like 'that', then the beginning needs to be 'this', and the next step 'so'. It's like a puzzle. But you can 'cheat' by looking at the end in order to find out how to solve it. From end to start to middle is a good way to proceed.

In a sense, it is very easy for me to work in Peter Brook's productions because he provides the actors with lots of material to stimulate their imaginations. All kinds of material. photographs, music, history, case studies, direct experiences, even food. Through this information, without being aware of it, you digest the world of the play. Then, when you start to work on the actual scenes, the material you have studied somehow re-emerges without your needing to think about it. You feel that you know what is going on, so you don't have to think about how to perform the scene: you are simply 'there'. You have something inside, and as a result the acting feels like an improvisation. Of course, you always follow the text, and you respect the stage directions, but at the same time you feel that you truly know what is happening.

When you are preparing a role, instead of worrying about how to speak the lines, or where to move, it is better to immerse yourself in the world of the play and the character. Get as much information as possible. Read books, but also talk to people, look at photographs or paintings, visit the landscape/setting of the play, and so on. If you work on the text in isolation, it doesn't mean anything. The words of the text are only a very small part of the character you are portraying, or the story that is being told. The text is like the tip of the iceberg; it is the bit you see, while under the surface there is a huge mass which goes unnoticed. If you try to get a sense of your role from the text alone, you will find it very limiting. It isn't enough. You need to discover all the rest of the material that is not set out in the script. If you do this first, then the text will simply emerge when the time comes to rehearse.

You might think that it is important to hold the audience's full attention at every single moment, but this is not the case. It isn't possible for people to sustain a high level of concentration for an hour or more, and so you have to find ways of giving them some relaxation from time to time. Actors have to offer the onlookers moments of 'air' even in the middle of the most intense production.

I discovered this when I was learning the technique of traditional storytelling. My teacher never gave me advice about how to perform well, but occasionally he would say, 'At this point in the recitation, you need to perform badly.'

In fact, you don't need to think about how to 'play well'. This is what you do as a matter of course. But sometimes you have to find when just to play in a very ordinary way.

If you are always 'good', the audience will be constantly straining to concentrate on your words. After a while they will get tired, and will fail to respond to what is actually being said.

In addition, if everything is equally 'good', the audience will soon become accustomed to it, and the key moments in the performance will not stand out. They will lose their impact. This same loss of responsiveness happens in cookery. If a host prepares a superb meal for his guests, they will begin by saying, 'This is utterly delicious!' But if every course the cook prepares is equally complex and superb, after a while it will fail to register. A smart cook will follow a rich, unusual dish with something simple and everyday, in order to cleanse the palate and reawaken the tastebuds. In the same way, the actor should not overburden the audience with a consistently brilliant performance. There needs to be moments where you 'perform badly' in order to reawaken their ability to appreciate and respond.

Obviously, when I say 'perform badly', I do not mean that you should give a truly horrible, egotistic, or shoddy performance. Merely that some moments need to be more ordinary and 'throwaway'. For example, if you are working on a long monologue, you start your preparation by discovering how it begins, how it then develops, and how it comes to an ending. The next stage is to decide which are the key phrases. These are important and must be played very well. Then you look at the lines before the key phrases. These must not be overemphasised or they will reduce the impact of what follows. You should try to speak these lines in an 'ordinary' way. Otherwise the audience will not be able to move with you through the speech, and will not respond to the important moments.

In the Japanese language, there is a word *ma*, which refers to 'emptiness' of both time and space. *Ma* contains 'nothing'; it is the moment where you refrain from saying or doing anything. This concept is extremely useful for theatre, since the absence of activity can be employed to create a kind of 'frame' for highlighting important moments. These 'absences' of action should be seen as an integral part of the play, not just moments where 'nothing is happening'. Just as music is constructed from both sound and silence, so is acting.

Ma also implies 'appropriate relationship' between objects or events. A good actor can successfully manipulate *ma*. He can sense the proper relationship between two moments, two people, two actions, two sentences, two scenes, and between the audience and the stage. *Ma* is not static thing, it is about connections.

This awareness of contrast also operates when you employ pauses in your speech. If you hold a long pause, the next lines cannot be spoken slowly; they must be performed quite quickly. Otherwise you will lose your audience. (Imagine it: a long, slow speech, followed by a weighty pause, followed by yet another slow ponderous series of words . . .)

In all of my work I am attempting to find something 'rare and unique' (as Zeami describes it). Convention is the enemy of the actor, and you have to work hard to avoid falling into the clichéd ways of playing a character. If this happens, you will not create a believable human being. You need to search for the subtleties and contradictions that give a sense of reality to your work. Conventional characters are one-dimensional. Real people are complex and riddled with contradictions. Equally, you must not try to do something totally outrageous simply in order to be different. It's not variety for the sake of variety.

Several years ago, I played Gonzalo in Peter Brook's production of *The Tempest*. When you read the text, you realise that all the other characters in the play describe Gonzalo as being kind and wise. So here you have a very conventional image of 'the wise old man'. I had to find a way of portraying Gonzalo that was truthful, yet didn't simply set up the clichéd image. In the beginning, I had him reacting in ways that were not obviously kind or wise. As the play progressed, and the audience saw Gonzalo's actions and responses, they drew their own conclusions about what kind of man he was. In the end they decided that he was 'a wise old man', but they came to this opinion by themselves. Obviously, we all have ideas about how a wise old man would look and speak, and I deliberately attempted to avoid these conventional images. If I had portrayed Gonzalo in this way from the outset, the audience would simply have said, 'Oh, it's a wise old man,' and would have lost their curiosity about him and his actions.

Every single aspect of theatre must aim to be 'rare and unique', not just the acting. The production itself needs to have variety and unexpected contrasts. There need to be surprises, sudden shifts of direction, and unique moments. Once again this is not simply a case of using fancy tricks for their shock value, but of finding truly original ways of making the truth of the play come alive. Our aim is not to present a production that is rare and unique, but to use an approach that is rare and unique to illuminate the production. 'Rare and unique' are the means of telling the story, not the end result.

Zeami identified the importance of 'novelty'. He noted that in nature, nothing ever stays exactly the same. A tree produces blossom, then leaves, then fruit, and then it seems to 'die' for a while, until the blossom reappears the next spring. The emergence of fresh blossom strikes us as beautiful because it is new each time. If the tree was in bloom all year round, we would cease to be interested, however gorgeous the flowers. It is the same in theatre. As an actor, if you always use the same means of expression (however skilful), you will lose your ability to 'charm' the audience. You must not remain stuck in old patterns; you should keep looking for new ways to contact the audience.

I would like to make clear that the concept of 'novelty' does not mean that you search for weird, shocking, bizarre performances. It is not 'change for the sake of change'. Rather, it is finding ways to keep your work fresh and alive. From the audience's point of view,

Speaking** **111**

a play that has true 'novelty' won't necessarily appear strange and shocking. Instead the audience will be so absorbed and moved by what they are seeing, that they will be unaware of the fact that they have seen a good performance.

Zeami went so far as to say that if an audience becomes aware that they are watching a 'novel' performance, the actor is not truly skilled. The 'flower' of an actor's craft must be kept secret, and the ability to create novelty is part of that 'flower'. Nobody should be able to see what is really happening. If the spectators start thinking, 'This is really original,' or, 'What a skilful actor!' it is not the work of a first-rate performer.

A Zen master once went to see a performance given by a famous storyteller, since everyone was talking about how good he was. After the show, the storyteller heard that the Zen master had been in the audience, and went up to him to find out his opinion of the performance. The Zen master said, 'It was very good, but you are speaking with your mouth.'

The storyteller replied, 'Thank you for your suggestion. I would like to come and study with you.'

After he had been working with the Zen master for some time, the storyteller again asked for an opinion on his performance. The Zen master said, 'Good, now you are telling the story without using your tongue.'

5 Learning

In Japan there is a saying that it is better to spend three years looking for a good teacher than to occupy the same period of time doing exercises with someone inferior.

You have to train in order to develop, but you can't study with just anyone. You need to find the right teacher. It doesn't really matter which style or technique you learn. In fact, you could train in disciplines as different as aikido, judo, ballet, or mime, and gain equal benefit. This is because you are learning something beyond technique. When you study with your master, the skills are only the language of understanding, not the purpose. Because you are learning something beyond technique, the subject is less important.

In the martial arts, the stated purpose of training is 'freedom'. Nonetheless, this doesn't mean that the martial arts are automatically the best way to learn 'how to find freedom'. In fact, any physical training system can work. All of them are designed to help you experience how the body and the voice function, which in turn enables you to find freedom through physical activity.

Of course, psychoanalysis or intellectual clarity also help you to become free in your thinking. Movement is not the only way to become mentally free.

According to Zeami, it is useful to commence training in singing and dance at the age of seven (in the Western system of counting age, this would be six years), since at that age children are not self-conscious. They have no ambition, and no clearly defined sense of exhibitionism or 'being successful'. They do not feel pressurised and so when they perform something interesting emerges. A certain beauty.

Zeami called this quality hana, *the 'flower' of a performer, and included the sense of 'charm' and 'novelty' in its meaning. This 'charm' is not the same charm that we see in daily life, which is a type of social ease. Nor does it mean physical beauty. It refers specifically to a particular quality of the performer on stage. L.M.*

Zeami noted how this *hana* changes as the performer moves through the different stages of his or her career. He says that children have a 'natural flower' that makes almost anything they do interesting to watch, and that it continues up until the age of sixteen or seventeen.

There is an old actor's saying that, 'You should never perform with animals and children, because they will always upstage you.' They are certainly fascinating to watch, but why is our eye caught and held by them? It is a bit of a mystery.

Zeami noted that during the early teens, a performer can probably demonstrate a certain level of technical mastery (if he or she has commenced training at five or six), and this, combined with their natural 'flower', enables them to be quite watchable. As a young actor, your 'charm' disguises weak points in the performance. Nonetheless, you must be careful not to take it too seriously if someone exclaims at the beauty of your acting, since all young actors have this 'charm'. You must not be seduced into believing that you are God's gift to the theatre. Instead, you need to really concentrate on developing your technique: how to strengthen and extend the voice, how to use the body, since the charm you have have depended on for so long is about to vanish.

When you reach the age of sixteen or so, you hit a difficult period theatrically. Visually and vocally you appear to be an adult: your body has altered and your voice has either changed or is in the process of changing. Similarly, your thinking patterns are more adult. Consequently, the audience will perceive you as an adult and judge your work accordingly. They will expect to see a polished performance, and you are not technically capable of delivering it. You have lost the 'flower' of childhood, but have not yet fully mastered your craft as a professional. It is a very awkward period, and the most useful thing to do at this point is simply to concentrate on your training. If you find yourself performing badly, don't worry too much, just keep on working.

This difficult period comes to an end around twenty-three or twenty-four, when you enter the most important stage of your professional life. By now your body has virtually finished growing and changing, and you are able to 'digest' physically whatever you have learnt. Your training and your physical development have come together, like a fruit that has ripened. At that age, if you perform in a young role, such as Romeo or Juliet, many people will be impressed and believe you to be a very good actor. It is true that you will look better and perhaps more convincing in that role compared to an older actor, but you shouldn't get too carried away by this success. It is merely a kind of coincidence: being in the right role at the right time. It isn't a measure of skilled acting. When people say that you are good at that age, it is possibly true that you have talent, but you must learn to look at it objectively. If you get carried away with the idea that you are a theatrical genius, you will lose whatever talent you have. You have to look at what you have done objectively, rather than subjectively. If you do so, you will quickly understand how your early success is a kind of coincidence, and that there is no guarantee that it will remain or continue.

Zeami considered the age of thirty-three or thirty-four to be the richest period in an actor's life. You can see the results of all your training, and if you have attained a certain standard or recognition in your work, it will be permanent. It is equally true that if you are still working as a second-rank actor at this age, it is unlikely to change in the future. At twenty-four anything is possible: you can suddenly transform from a mediocre to an excellent actor; but after thirty-four miracles rarely happen. You must be very honest with yourself and objectively analyse your abilities. In addition, if you haven't achieved technical mastery of your art at that age, you have a problem. In about ten years your physical skills will start to decline (around the age of forty-five), so if you haven't got your technique firmly under your belt by thirty-five you will have very little to work with. If, at thirty-five, you are able to 'charm' the audience, this is the real flower of your art. Not the flower of youth or coincidence, but the genuine article.

However, if you cannot find this 'charm' by the age of thirty-five, you should consider your future very carefully. Either you will have to concentrate on your work with twice as much effort, or you should give up. Apart from anything else, you have to realistically examine where and how you can be cast in order to continue working in theatre.

Zeami noted that around forty-three or forty-four you hit another change. Your physical beauty is starting to decline, and your body's energy begins to run out. While you can do extravagant, extraordinary feats of skill at the age of thirty-four with relative ease, you can't do the same actions in the same way at the age of forty-four. This doesn't mean that you have nothing to offer the audience. Instead of demonstrating your technical prowess, you focus on exactly what you are saying or doing. You reduce the outside expression but retain the integrity of your actions. You are no longer dependent on physical beauty, but the audience still senses something delicate and moving that comes from inside. This again is a 'real flower' of the actor's art. Zeami also commented that at this age it is important to analyse carefully what you can and can't do. And to start teaching. This combination of self-analysis and the nourishing of younger actors (and the inevitable dialogue that occurs between these two activities) will keep you developing as a performer right into your old age.

After the age of fifty, Zeami felt that it was almost impossible for an actor to physically reproduce what he had done in the past. At this age, the ability to hold the audience's attention cannot depend on exterior skills. Instead you must base your performance on something which is interior: the 'invisible' part of acting. If this exists, the audience's attention will remain focused on your performance. If an actor has learned real, true acting over all the years prior to the fifties, then even if the tree is old, a bit bent and gnarled, it will still be able to produce a flower. This will not be an extravagant 'charm', but rather a deep and enduring beauty. In an older actor who is truly skilled, the voice might be weak, the body unable to sustain strong activity, yet there will be *something* interesting, compelling, charming and moving about their work. In this case the acting is almost entirely 'interior'.

At this point I should remind the reader that these ideas about theatre were expressed by Zeami over five hundred years ago, and referred only to male actors (since women were forbidden to perform at that period in Japanese history). They are obviously still relevant today, with a couple of exceptions. According to my own observation, the transition points for women tend to occur slightly earlier than for men. It is also useful to remind yourselves that the theatre he is describing is very physical, in some ways more like dance than conventional text-based theatre.

In addition, modern health and nutrition has generally improved both the length and the quality of human life since then, and this needs to be taken into account. Fifty years was true old age at the time when he was writing, and this is no longer the case. Observation suggests that the periods in later life that he refers to need to be adjusted upwards by about ten years. When he speaks about an actor of forty-five it more accurately refers to an actor of fifty-five in the modern world, and so on. The earlier years (teens up to forty) seem to be more or less the same nowadays. If anything, these ages should be adjusted downwards by a year or so (sixteen meaning a modern fourteen or fifteen). This is also due to the effect of better nutrition producing earlier physical maturity. This is a much smaller discrepancy, and on the whole Zeami's observations are still as relevant today as when he wrote them.

I once heard a story about a brilliant tightrope walker who worked in a circus. After one of his habitually polished perform-ances he turned to the audience and said, 'I have a son who is six years old. For the last two years he has been studying how to walk the tightrope. I would like to present him to you tonight as he makes his debut in front of an audience. Of course you can't expect him to be highly skilled, but please make him feel welcome.'

The child then came out and started his short walk on the wire. He had a lot of difficulty balancing; at one point he almost fell off, but somehow managed to recover. Eventually he made it to the other end of the rope, to be greeted by a wave of applause. This was genuine applause not just for the successful completion of the task, but because he had managed to capture and hold the audience's attention for the duration of his performance. In fact, in some ways, his performance was more 'interesting' than his father's. Obviously whatever rendered his performance fascinating to watch wasn't technical mastery or the creation of a 'new style' of tightrope walk-ing. It was something else. The child had his whole life in the performance; the father only had his superb technique.

A Zen master once noted that, from the moment of birth, each human being contains a 'seed', which can eventually grow and transform into the 'flower' of divinity. Thinking about the divine acts as a kind of 'rain' which enables the seed to sprout and grow. The understanding of divinity is the 'flower', which in turn produces the 'fruit' of enlightenment. This is the same 'flower' as the actor's 'flower'. Once you have started your studies in your childhood, each age brings new and deeper understanding of what it means to be an actor. You look at yourself objectively, analyse your craft, train, search yourself, study, and then when the 'flower' opens, you struggle to maintain it. You continue to nurture it, so that it doesn't wither away and die.

But in order to produce a beautiful flower, you have to know what the seed consists of. I believe that the beautiful 'flower' emerges from the opening of the heart. A beautiful 'flower' depends on how you move your inner being. You must discover how this operates, since the quality of your acting reflects this. Even if your body is withered and old, something very beautiful and clear can emerge, if you have maintained a strong and open heart. This goes beyond technique.

Zeami offers three concepts to define the actor's craft. He describes these elements as 'skin', 'flesh' and 'bone'. The skin is the exterior beauty of the actor, the flesh is the beauty that comes through training, and bone is the essential nature of the person, a kind of spiritual beauty. Certain actors are born with an innate quality, which is the skeleton of their craft. Then training provides the flesh, and what finally appears on the outside, to an audience, is the skin.

Another way of describing this is 'looking', 'hearing', and 'feeling'. The audience looks at the actor; the beauty you see is 'skin'. Then the musicality of the performance, the timing, and harmony of expression that you hear is the 'flesh'. Finally, the actor's performance moves you on a deep, almost metaphysical level: you feel something very profound. This is the 'bone' of the artist's craft. On the stage is the beauty of the body, the beauty of the performance, and the beauty of the mind that has created the performance. To be a good actor, each of these elements needs to be maintained at the highest level.

When I talk about the 'beauty', I do not mean 'prettiness' or fashionable beauty. If your spirit ('bone') is beautiful, this is what will appear on the surface.

There was once a young samurai who studied extremely hard, and people started saying how good he was. They noted that he was highly skilled, since he had clearly acquired a lot of technique. One day, after practising at the dojo, he went to a restaurant where he had a meal and drank a cup of rice wine. Eventually he left to go home, but by this time it was very dark and he couldn't see anything in front of him. However, since he had developed his awareness and sensitivity as part of his samurai training, he was able to make his way along the road. He eventually came to a river, and as he was crossing the bridge, he bumped into somebody. He immediately reached for his sword, but it was too late; another sword was already at his throat. There was nothing he could do.

Eventually the other man said, 'I heard that you are supposed to be a famous fighter, but that can't be true. You aren't strong enough. You aren't capable of defending yourself against my sword. You've acquired a lot of technique, and you are satisfied with that. You are totally useless. It would be better if I just killed you now.'

The sword bit deeper into his neck. And then, in a completely unexpected move, the young samurai jumped into the river. It was the middle of winter, and the water was freezing, but he managed to save his life. He yelled back at his attacker, 'You are very strong, please tell me your name.'

The stranger responded, 'No, I don't want to tell you my name. But if you are starting to feel shamed by this encounter, I'll give you some advice. Train your inner being. Technique is not enough. If you can manage to go beyond technique you will be very strong, but at the moment you are satisfied with your technical understanding, and you think that this makes you proficient. That's wrong. You must go beyond technique.'

'What is beyond technique?'

'Another existence. Inside your physical existence is another existence. When you meet with this you will understand.'

With this, the stranger departed. The young samurai scrambled out of the river, and made the decision to study in a Zen monastery.

I don't really believe you can learn 'acting'. There may be some techniques that will help you create a performance under specific circumstances, for example, how to be good on television, or to perform in a highly codified style such as Kabuki or Peking Opera, but these are only effective in that particular context. In fact, each production requires its own method of performance. Also, if you are involved in creating a totally new piece of theatre, you will have to create a new kind of acting to match.

Since each production demands its own personal 'acting method', it is difficult to teach 'acting method' as a general skill. In addition, as an artist, you have to be willing to destroy previous methods of performing, in order to create what is needed here and now. When you are actually on stage, you must forget about all the theories, all the philosophies, all the interesting techniques. Just do it.

Before I commenced my career, I thought that I was incredibly talented. I believed that I could become the finest actor in Japan. Unfortunately, as I started to get regular work, people began telling me that I really wasn't very good. In fact, I was dreadful. It was quite a blow to discover that I wasn't the genius of my dreams, but, having begun to work in theatre, I felt I should stick with it. This was partly pride; I didn't want to admit that I had made a mistake in my choice of career. At the same time, I felt great despair as I realised that I really wasn't particularly talented. Nonetheless, I continued. And I started to think. If I didn't have talent, what else was there?

I couldn't 'get' genius, but I could get training. I began to work hard, and tried to become as skilled as possible. After a while, people came up to me and said that I still wasn't very good, and I should consider getting out of theatre. Of course, they acknowledged that I was hard-working and dedicated, but unfortunately I just wasn't that interesting to watch.

A few years later, I was on the verge of quitting. I accepted the fact that I wasn't a good actor, and realised that I had little chance of success. And, of course, that was the moment when people finally began saying that my work really wasn't too bad after all.

The *Mahabharata* was Peter Brook's big project, lasting over four years. I was really interested in it, and wanted to see how Peter would bring the complex world of the story into the theatre. Once again I decided I had better keep on acting, otherwise I wouldn't be able to witness the way the project developed.

For me the rehearsal process was wonderful. It was fascinating to observe how a great director worked on a piece of this magnitude. I enjoyed every moment of the rehearsals. Unfortunately, after ten months, they came to an end, the production was ready, and now I had to get on with the job of acting. After the good times came the bad: two years playing the same thing, day after day.

If I had played it in the same fashion every single day, I would have gone mad with boredom. To avoid this problem, I decided to try another way of acting. I decided I wouldn't think about whether I was good or bad, I would simply try to enjoy myself on stage. Every day, in a sense egotistically, I tried to find the pleasure in my performance. And people suddenly said that I was much better than before.

Then I worked on *The Man Who*. In this play, I changed again. I didn't care whether I was enjoying myself or not. I didn't care about the fact that I was repeating the same performance time after time. In fact I didn't care about anything. Instead I focused on the details: right hand up, head turns, pronounce one line, then the next one. Like a ritual. A ritual of daily life.

I find it quite similar to the traditional tea ceremony. In the tea ceremony, there are a lot of complex details. Every action has a prescribed pattern. How you wipe the cup, how you light the fire, how you pour the water: it is all carefully choreographed. You follow this complicated order to produce a cup of tea that you give to your guests. In fact you have done nothing special; just made a cup of tea. It is nothing fantastic, but it gives you great pleasure to prepare and serve it.

Once I did the tea ceremony in front of a great master. For some reason, I suddenly felt an enormous affection towards the green powder of the tea, and crushed it very gently, with a lot of love. This feeling of love and affection continued through the rest of the ceremony. I listened to the sound of the water boiling. I noticed the change in tone when I added cold water. Eventually I gave the cup to the master, who said, 'Now, this looks like delicious tea.'

A student of sword fighting was practising one day, when his teacher came up to him and commented, 'You are quite good, but somehow it isn't enough. There is something missing.'

The student thought very hard about what his master had said, but couldn't make any sense of the remark. A few days later he approached the teacher and said, 'I haven't been able to find out what was missing. Obviously there is some great secret of the art of the sword which I am unable to understand.'

With that, he decided there was no point worrying about how he should manipulate the sword. He discarded thoughts of his weapon and just stood there looking at this teacher. Normally in Japan, when you face a great master, he seems very big while you feel quite small. But in this case, the young man suddenly felt that his sense if his own body was enormous, while his teacher appeared to shrink. At that moment, the master smiled, and said, 'Now you've got it! You have found the secret of fighting.'

It can only happen when you 'throw away the sword'.

This 'inner emptiness' is a nice aim, but how do we get there? Unfortunately, there is no map or guidebook, and you can only see how you got there after your arrival.

When you look back, you can say, 'Oh, that was a real turning point,' or, 'This is the phrase that suddenly altered my priorities.' Or, 'I thought I was doing this, but in fact I was doing that,' or even, 'What a lot of tiny events conspired to bring me here. I never noticed at the time.' And this is what happens; while you are walking the path, you can't see it. It is only with hindsight that the pattern becomes clear. L.M.

When I speak about 'self-learning', I am not talking about an intellectual programme of training, rather a general openness and willingness to move onwards. It is responsiveness, not rigidity.

A Chinese sage was answering his student's questions. One of the questions was, 'What am I?'

The sage replied, 'You are a plate.'

In Eastern religious ceremonies a special plate is used to hold the offerings made to the gods. The plate supports the precious objects. The sage chose the symbols of 'plate' and 'offerings', to clarify the difference between *Yu* (existence) and *Mu* (nothingness). *Yu* is like 'phenomenon'; it is the visible effect of action. We see it, hear it, recognise it. It is like the precious objects offered to the gods. *Mu* is like 'form'; it is difficult to detect, yet it gives rise to the diversity of phenomenon. In describing his student as a plate, the sage was reminding him of this deeper level of existence. In the same way, the invisible part of the actor is the plate that gives rise to and supports the visible action of the performance. You don't notice its presence. Only its absence.

Consider the Heart Sutra in Buddhism. It says: 'phenomenon is emptiness and emptiness is phenomenon'. In a sense, everything arises from 'emptiness' or 'nothingness'. You admire the beauty of blossoms on a tree. But if you slash open the tree to discover what creates this beauty, you will find 'nothing': no baby blossoms or magical patterns, just hard wood. If you think about nature in all its glory and diversity, you are amazed. Trees, flowers, snow, sea, grass. These are all manifestations of what we call nature, but what is nature itself? Where is it? It can't be found. It is the 'nothingness' that gives rise to countless 'phenomena'. We can look at acting in the same way. Like nature, the heart of the actor can give life to virtually anything. Like nature, it is a kind of fertile nothingness.

As an actor, you must be a bit careful when dealing with all these concepts of 'nothingness' and 'phenomena'. These are intellectual concepts, and if you cling too tightly to them they can lead you astray. If you are consciously thinking about 'emptiness' then it is not real 'emptiness'; it is an idea labelled 'emptiness'. As such, it is only another kind of 'phenomenon'. Real emptiness is beyond thought and is limitlessly free. Being attached to the concept of 'emptiness', or constantly thinking about achieving 'nothingness' is just another prison or constraint on your acting.

All of this is difficult to understand and tricky to put into practice. 'Nothingness' is beyond thought, but how can we achieve it without thinking about it? Perhaps we should just focus on something Zeami said: '*Yuu raku shu do fu ken,*' which translates as: 'Play around freely, study the path, and you will see the wind.'

Effort, training, study and work are what you concentrate on. After a long period of slog, a kind of freedom emerges. You no longer think about what you are doing, or how you are achieving your effects. The performance simply happens. This freedom is the actor's 'nothingness'. At the highest level it is like being a baby; nothing is planned or consciously constructed, but your thoughts and feelings emerge with vitality and total clarity.

In medieval Japan, there was a famous warrior called Musashi Miyamoto. He was known for using a wooden practice sword (instead of a real blade), even when his opponents attacked with steel weapons. He was even more famous for winning under these circumstances. After one such duel, someone asked why he had chosen to use a wooden sword instead of a real one. Musashi replied, 'If I had used a real weapon, I wouldn't have taken the duel seriously enough. I would have depended on the blade to do the work for me. In fact, my presence would hardly have been necessary. It would have been as if I wasn't there or didn't exist. But with a wooden sword, my interior has to be really concentrated and strong. This is why I prefer it.'

As well as being a superb fighter, Musashi Miyamoto spent years studying the principles and philosophy of the martial arts. After many years he concluded that, 'Every system, every thought, every technique, and every philosophical concept points to the same emptiness. Everything is one emptiness.'

Of course, nobody could understand what he was talking about. 'Emptiness' is very hard to explain. It is the same in Zen meditation. Practitioners occasionally experience something called *satori*, which is equally impossible to describe.

When we speak about teaching, it is simply someone else's experience. Your teacher has walked the path ahead of you, and you look at their tracks in the dust. They might provide you with some hints about where to go next. But these 'tracks' are somebody else's past, they are not your future. All the books and courses are simply maps of other people's pasts. Absorb and use them, but always remember that your own path will be different, and it is this personal path that you must travel. Don't try to exactly copy another person's path; use their knowledge, but remain aware that the particular 'landscape' of your own path is unique. However, the paradox remains: you must discover your own path, but you can't perceive it while you are on it, only after you have travelled it.

In this book, I talk a lot about what various people have said. But you shouldn't just accept everything that is written here without question. In fact, if you believe every single thing you read, it is better not to read at all.

There was a famous Kabuki actor, who died about fifty years ago, who said, 'I can teach you the gesture pattern that indicates "looking at the moon". I can teach you the movement up to the tip of the finger which points to the sky. From the tip of your finger to the moon is your own responsibility.'